30 Second Devotional
for First Responders

30 Second Devotional
for First Responders

Barry Young

ISBN (Print): 978-1-54395-002-1
ISBN (eBook): 978-1-54395-003-8

Dedication

This book is dedicated to the two fathers God has so graciously given to me!

I am forever grateful for my father, Staff Sgt. Thomas Richard Young, of the United States Marine Corps. My father served in World War II and the Korean War. Not only was he a powerful warrior for the United States, but he was also a mighty warrior for Jesus. I love you, Dad!

I am also incredibly thankful for my father-in-law, Captain Stephen Terry Faries, of the United States Army. He has shown me the love of God in so many ways. He constantly demonstrates by his example the undeserved, gracious, love of our heavenly father. I love you, Dad!

Acknowledgment

I WANT TO GIVE special thanks to Vaughn and Glenda Baker as well as Mark and Leanda Warren. It is such a blessing and honor to work with them and Strategos International. Because of their efforts, countless lives have been saved and protected through the many trainings and programs Strategos provides worldwide.

I want to express my thanks to all the Serving Pastors Ministry supporters and monthly partners. Kelly and I are able to share the gospel all over the nation because of your prayers and support. You are making an eternal difference. From the bottom of our hearts, we love you and thank you!

Lastly, I am incredibly grateful for my beloved wife, Kelly. Her contribution to the ministry and most importantly my life are invaluable. Kelly, I love you with all of my heart and I can't put into words how thankful I am for you.

Facts About Your Life

§

SCIENCE CAN'T ANSWER THE three most important questions we have in life. Where did we come from? Why are we here? Where will we go when we die? Friend, it isn't an accident that this book is in your hand. One day you are going to die, and so will I. Are you walking with God? Are you right with God? Have you asked his son, Jesus Christ, into your life? There is absolutely no way you, by yourself, can earn eternal life! The Bible clearly states in Romans 3:23, "All have sinned." The Bible also clearly states in Romans 6:23, "For the wages of sin is death." We will all die, and if we do not receive the gift of eternal life found only in Jesus, we have nothing to look forward to but physical death and then an eternity separated from God. There is, however, hope!

PRAYER OF SALVATION

Having eternal life with God is not about a religion; it is not about a specific church, and it is certainly not about the efforts of man. Having eternal life is about a person, Jesus Christ. If you would like to receive Jesus Christ as Lord, he can save you, forgive you, heal you, love you, and most importantly, give you eternal life. The Bible says in Romans 10:9-10, "If you declare with your mouth, 'Jesus is Lord,' and believe in your heart that God raised him from the dead, you will be saved. For it is with your heart that you believe and are justified, and it is with your mouth that you profess your faith and are saved." If you would like to receive eternal life, would you pray this prayer?

Lord Jesus, right now, I call on your name. I ask you to be the Lord of my life. I ask you to forgive me for all of my sins. I confess with my mouth and I believe in my heart that you died on the cross and rose from the grave. I receive your love and your salvation.

Friend, if you prayed that prayer in faith, you are now a Christian. If you are not in a Bible-believing church, start attending one now. As believers, we need one another. If you prayed this prayer, would you contact our ministry at www.servingpastors.com? We would love to hear your story.

Introduction

§

I AM SO GLAD you are holding this book in your hand. To every first responder, thank you for your service! As a first responder, God has used you and your hands to bless and protect so many people. If you are reading this book, just know I have prayed for you. I have prayed that God would use this book to bless, empower, and encourage you and every first responder to live a life filled with the power, purpose, and love for God.

The goal of this book is not for people to spend 30 seconds with God and stop. No, quite the contrary. Statistics show that an overwhelming majority of Christians do not spend daily time with God. Oftentimes, spending daily time with God is referred to as a quiet time or devotional time. The key to believers having blessed lives, forming healthy relationships, and becoming all that God wants them to be simply rests in spending time with God!

The purpose of this book is to get every reader spending daily time with God. Thirty seconds a day with God is not the finish line; it is the starting line. Listen to this scripture from Psalm 34:8, "Taste and see that the Lord is good; blessed is the one who takes refuge in him." My goal is for readers of this book to taste and see that the Lord is good and want more of him.

I believe if you will start spending 30 seconds with God daily for an entire year, then the goodness of God will overwhelm you. The more time you spend with God, the more you will want to meet with Him on a regular basis. I believe 30 seconds with God can turn into a daily, intimate meeting between a loving heavenly Father and his child. I believe that daily intimate meetings will turn into a life full of God's promises fulfilled and amazing adventures lived.

God has amazing plans for your life! God wants to do more in your life than you can imagine. In John 10:10 Jesus said, "I have come that they may have life, and have it to the full." The only way to have abundant life is to spend daily time with the author of life. God loves you, and so do I. Be blessed!

Barry

JANUARY 1ST

James 4:7 —"Submit yourselves, then, to God. Resist the devil, and he will flee from you."

Have you ever noticed how people sometimes misquote this verse? Often, people say the key to spiritual victory is resisting the devil. However, this statement is incorrect! If we want real supernatural power and authority, we have to first submit to God and then resist the devil. Many times, our culture suffers from a submission problem. We have to submit to God first and foremost. None of us have true power to resist the devil until we have first submitted our days, lives, and dreams to God.

RESPONDER'S REFLECTION: If you want God to do amazing things in your life, it is directly tied into your ability to submit to him.

JANUARY 2ND

James 1:22 —"Do not merely listen to the word, and so deceive yourselves. Do what it says."

Do you want everything God wants you to have? Do you want to live each day in the supernatural power of God? If you want everything God wants you to have, you need to do everything God wants you to do! God does not save us until we call out to him. God does not forgive us until we repent and ask for his forgiveness. If we want to see the Lord do amazing and mighty things in our lives, there is a price to pay.

RESPONDER'S REFLECTION: If you want everything God wants you to have, you need to do everything God wants you to do.

JANUARY 3RD

Ephesians 1:19-20 —"His incomparably great power for us who believe. That power is the same as the mighty strength he exerted when he raised Christ from the dead and seated him at his right hand in the heavenly realms."

God has given you all the power you need to change your world and the lives of those around you. Everything you need is in you! According to this verse, the power that raised Jesus from the dead is the same power at work in those whose faith is in Jesus! What more do you need? God wants to use you to do mighty exploits. Do not wait until you get further understanding, better training, or take that class before you believe God for big things. God wants to use you right now. You have everything you need to change the world. If your faith is in Jesus, the power of his resurrection is in you!

RESPONDER'S REFLECTION: If the devil is not able to convince you to give up on your dream, then he will simply try to get you to postpone it. Tap into God's power to fulfill that dream!

JANUARY 4TH

2 Corinthians 9:10 —"Now he who supplies seed to the sower and bread for food will also supply and increase your store of seed and will enlarge the harvest of your righteousness."

The expression "bloom where you are planted" offers some of the greatest advice I have ever heard. Sometimes we can have so much regret about the past that we let go of the future. On the other hand, if we are not careful, we can let the worries of tomorrow steal today. Friend, God wants you focused on today. Be excited about where you are at now. Live life in the present. Wherever God has you, bloom where you are planted.

RESPONDER'S REFLECTION: Reflect on this great quote from Bil Keane, "Yesterday is history, tomorrow is a mystery, today is a gift of God, which is why we call it the present."

JANUARY 5TH

Proverbs 30:32 —"If you play the fool and exalt yourself, or if you plan evil, clap your hand over your mouth!"

Sadly, I can relate to this verse because at times, I have played the fool and exalted myself. I have a feeling if you are honest with yourself, you could probably say the same thing. When we exalt ourselves or become selfish, we will grow powerless. If you want more of God's power to live, love, and endure, you have to place God and others before yourself. I once heard a phrase worth mentioning that states, "No man is more empty who is full of himself."

RESPONDER'S REFLECTION: The more focused you are on yourself, the less power you will have from God. The more focused you are on putting God first, the more his supernatural power will flow into your life.

JANUARY 6TH

Psalm 144:1 —"Praise be to the Lord my Rock, who trains my hands for war, my fingers for battle."

God has not called you to be overcome, but to be an overcomer. However, if you want God's very best for your life, you have to fight for it! Consider the following attributes of a warrior:

1. Warriors do not quit!
2. Warriors worship God despite the trials they are facing.
3. Warriors refuse to let the words of their detractors stop them from the mission.
4. Warriors use negative experiences to motivate them to win.

Today, reflect on the truth that God calls you to be a victorious warrior and champion!

RESPONDER'S REFLECTION: You cannot win a battle you are unwilling to fight.

JANUARY 7TH

Exodus 17:12 — "When Moses' hands grew tired, they took a stone and put it under him and he sat on it. Aaron and Hur held his hands up—one on one side, one on the other—so that his hands remained steady till sunset."

In this story, God's people were under attack and every time Moses raised his hands, God's people would win the battle. If he lowered his hands, God's people would begin to lose the battle. Have you ever considered that your success requires the aid of others? If we go it alone, we will lose alone. However, the opposite is true, if we go together, we will win together. If you are struggling in life, do not go to battle alone! We need others to accomplish our goals and to have God's victory and blessing in our lives.

RESPONDER'S REFLECTION: We are stronger together. If we go it alone, we will lose every time.

JANUARY 8TH

Lucas 1:37—"Porque para Dios no hay nada imposible."

If you do not understand Spanish, the above scripture says, "For with God nothing is impossible." In the same way that we might struggle to understand a different language, we may not always fully comprehend what God is saying when he speaks to us. Friend, God wants to do amazing things in your life today. His desire to bless you is so vast that you may not be able to understand it at first. True faith in God is taking that first step even when he has not revealed all the remaining steps.

RESPONDER'S REFLECTION: Just because you can't understand God doesn't mean he isn't speaking to you.

JANUARY 9TH

John 10:10 —"I have come that they may have life, and have it to the full."

Everyone may want to have an abundant life, but not everybody wants to do what it takes to have this life. If you want an abundant life, you have to live an obedient life. If you want the overflow of God's favor and power, you have to do things God's way and not your own. We cannot be the ones in control of our lives if we want to have God's very best.

RESPONDER'S REFLECTION: If you want an abundant life, you have to live an obedient life! There are no short cuts to living a life of obedience to God. Where is it in your life that you need to start obeying God?

JANUARY 10TH

Proverbs 21:26 —"All day long he craves for more, but the righteous give without sparing."

Has God asked you to give up something? Oftentimes, this thought can be scary. The devil wants us to fight God when he asks us to give that something up. However, ponder this thought —When God asks you to surrender, it is not because he wants to take something from you, it is because he wants to give you something better. If you are in the wrong place, you could miss the right opportunity. If you have friends who drag you down, you could miss the promotion of a lifetime. If God is asking you to hand something over to him, trust that he wants to prosper and favor you.

RESPONDER'S REFLECTION: When God asks you to give up something, it is not because he wants to take something from you; it is because he wants to give something to you. When God asks us for something, his motivation for that request is always for our good!

JANUARY 11TH

Isaiah 55:8 — "'For my thoughts are not your thoughts, neither are your ways my ways,' declares the Lord."

How do you know if God has moved in a person's life? The answer is simply, if God did it, you can't explain it! God wants to move in your life in such a powerful and loving way that you can't describe it. He wants to exceed your expectations. Isn't this what people do when they are in love with each other? Guess what, God is in love with you! Don't limit yourself and don't limit God. He has indescribable plans and desires for you!

RESPONDER'S REFLECTION: If God did it, you can't explain it! God has amazing plans for your life!

JANUARY 12TH

Galatians 6:7 — "A man reaps what he sows."

If you sow a sinful thought, you will reap a sinful action.
If you sow a sinful action, you will reap a sinful habit.
If you sow a sinful habit, you will reap a sinful character.
If you sow a sinful character, you will reap a sinful destiny.

RESPONDER'S REFLECTION: The way to prevent destruction in our lives is to sow God's thoughts and words into our minds. You can't change your life until you change your thinking. The only person who can control your thinking is you.

JANUARY 13TH

Joshua 24:15 — "Then choose for yourselves this day whom you will serve."

If you want to change your life, change your choices. Life is about choices. Martin Luther King, Jr. once said, "The time is always right to do what is right." The vast majority of people who are blessed have made the decision to be blessed. Your choices will either push you forward or they will pull you back. The choice to be successful, powerful, and significant is yours. God wants your life to live longer than you do. If your choices line up with God and his word you can't help but live an abundant life. Today, make your choices in light of eternity.

RESPONDER'S REFLECTION: If you want to change your life, change your choices. Many times good choices are tough today but they bring blessings tomorrow.

JANUARY 14TH

Proverbs 16:3 — "Commit to the Lord whatever you do, and he will establish your plans."

Today is an opportunity for your dreams and desires to become reality. I want to encourage you to live life at full throttle. This year don't hold back. Step out in faith and go all in on what God has for you. Don't watch other people walk in God's power; you walk in God's power. Don't merely be a spectator, but become an active participant in the amazing journey of life. God has supernatural plans for your life, but in order for his plans to transpire, you have to partner with God!

RESPONDER'S REFLECTION: Don't watch other people walk in God's power; you walk in God's power. Do something today that you have dreamed of doing, but never had the guts to try!

JANUARY 15TH

Proverbs 18:21 —"Death and life are in the power of the tongue."

You can't have a positive life and a negative mouth! So many times, other people's words can hurt us. Sadly, and perhaps even more often, we get hurt by our own words. The moment you say, "I can't do it" you have just made your vision harder to accomplish. The moment you declare, "I will never overcome this pain" you have just put a roadblock in front of yourself. Today, would you boldly declare God's promises over every area of your life regardless of what you see in front of you? God is for you but you have to be for yourself as well!

RESPONDERS REFLECTION: You cannot have a positive life and a negative mouth. Boldly declare God's promises over every area of your life regardless of what you see in front of you.

JANUARY 16TH

Romans 8:31 —"If God is for us, who can be against us?"

What a powerful thought that the Creator of the universe is for you! What does it matter if your boss, friends, neighbors, or the devil himself is against you, if God is for you? If God brings you to it, he will bring you through it. Your failures can't stop you. Your boss can't stop you. Your limitations can't stop you. Your fears can't stop you. Your financial situation can't stop you. Friend nothing can stop you when you realize the Creator of the world is for you!

RESPONDER'S REFLECTION: If God brings you to it, he will bring you through it. Don't get side tracked on what you can't do; instead consider what God can do. You can't change the world focusing on what you can't do, but you can change the world focusing on what God can do!

JANUARY 17TH

Psalm 103:12 — "As far as the east is from the west, so far has he removed our transgressions from us."

Sometimes our sins and failures can feel like flypaper! At times, we try to shake off a mistake we have made, but we just have trouble breaking free. Friend, I have good news. When we admit our sins to God, the most powerful force in the world steps between our transgressions and us: the LOVE of God! God wants you to know he has freed you from your past mishaps. God is giving you a new start called TODAY!

RESPONDER'S REFLECTION: You can only go so far north before you eventually start going south. However, you could travel a million miles east and would still never be going west. That is how far God has removed our sins from us!

JANUARY 18TH

1 Corinthians 15:57 — "He gives us the victory through our Lord Jesus Christ."

God wants you to be a victor. However, do you desire to be a champion? Being victorious requires making good choices daily. Champions don't just make choices they can enjoy today, but they also make ones they can benefit from tomorrow. As you contemplate the choices you will face today, don't make the easy choice, but instead make the right choice. Right choices can be difficult today, but will bring you blessings for many years to come.

RESPONDER'S REFLECTION: There are no shortcuts to victory in life. There are no shortcuts to an abundant life. There are no shortcuts to the supernatural life. Avoid taking shortcuts!

JANUARY 19TH

1 John 3:1 — "See what great love the Father has lavished on us."

Do you believe God is mad at you? Do you ever feel like you let God down? If you answered "yes" to these questions, you believe a lie. God is not mad at you; he is mad *about* you. God may be disappointed when we sin or fail but he is not disappointed in you. The Lord is not mad at you. One of the most vital keys to having a victorious life is to know that God loves you without conditions! God will never love you more than he does right now!

RESPONDER'S REFLECTION: God is not mad at you, God is mad about you! When you hear a voice saying the message that God is mad at you just know that voice is not coming from your heavenly father.

JANUARY 20TH

2 Chronicles 13:12 — "Do not fight against the Lord."

Sometimes in life, we fight the wrong person. For most of us, we may not intend to fight God, but there are times when we are opposing him. You might be thinking, "How do I fight God?" First, we battle God when we quarrel with other believers. Isn't it sad when Christians attack other Christians? Let me encourage you with this one phrase — save your bullets for the devil! Do not attack other believers verbally, physically, or in any other way. If you disagree with another Christian, just leave it at that and still love that person anyway. We are stronger when we are together!

RESPONDER'S REFLECTION: Save your bullets for the devil. Christians attacking other Christians is the friendly fire that makes us all weaker. Make sure your target is on the enemy himself, and not on other believers.

JANUARY 21ST

Psalm 121:1 — "I lift up my eyes."

What are you looking at today? Are you focusing on problems or opportunities? If we view our obstacles as problems, then we can plan to have a bad day. However, if we view our problems as opportunities, our day can go from negative to positive immediately! Today, I want to encourage you to lift up your eyes to the hope and possibility only God can give, and take your eyes off the problems you may face!

RESPONDER'S REFLECTION: The biggest problem God's people faced in the Old Testament was not the giants in the land. The biggest obstacle they faced was the attitude in their minds.

JANUARY 22ND

Matthew 6:5 — "And when you pray."

There is power in prayer! Oftentimes, we want to have microwave short prayers where we expect instant results. Can I give you one word to guide how you pray? PUSH!

P...pray
U...until
S...something
H...happens

I promise God loves you and he is listening. Just because there might be a delay with God, does not mean there is a denial.

RESPONDER'S REFLECTION: The most powerful weapon any Christian has is that of prayer. Are you daily using this weapon?

JANUARY 23RD

John 3:16 — "For God so loved the world that he gave his one and only Son."

We are never more like God than when we give. God is so many things but one of the chief characteristics about God is he is a giver! God gives life, hope, peace, strength, wisdom, and so much more. Today, if you want to touch someone's life, give! You can donate your money/resources to those in need or you can give your friendship to someone who needs a friend. Another way is to give of your time to mentor a young person who does not have a positive role model in his or her life. There are numerous ways to give and when we do, we partner with God to touch and change people's lives!

RESPONDER'S REFLECTION: We are never more like God than when we give. The natural response of man is to take. The natural response of God is to give. We need to be more like God.

JANUARY 24TH

Ephesians 2:14 — "For he himself is our peace."

Do you want more peace in your life? Anxiety, fear, and worry are based out of a life that is occupied with self. On the contrary, peace, joy, and contentment are based out of a life that is occupied with Jesus. Peace in life comes down to what we center our lives on, either Jesus or ourselves. When God is at the center of our lives, choices, and daily habits, peace will naturally overflow into every area of our being.

RESPONDER'S REFLECTION: Is your life primarily focused on self or on Jesus? Peace will overflow in your life when you allow Jesus to be in the center of your life.

JANUARY 25TH

1 John 4:4 — *"The one who is in you is greater than the one who is in the world."*

Greater is he who is in you than the:

1. Worry you are facing.
2. Past mistakes you have made.
3. Stress you are encountering today.
4. Fear you are confronting.
5. Financial pressure you are feeling.
6. Habits you are dealing with.
7. Job situation you are in.

RESPONDER'S REFLECTION: It doesn't take a lot of man if God has all the man. Don't focus on the size of your obstacles, focus on the size of your God.

JANUARY 26TH

Colossians 3:2 — *"Set your minds on things above, not on earthly things."*

How many times have you seen people preoccupied with texting while walking where they almost fall down or hit into someone or something? In our lives, when we go through our day strictly focused on and distracted by our hurts and issues, we become that person! However, when we lift our eyes above the problems and pains we are facing, that is when God can guide and direct us. Today, make sure to "set your mind on things above."

RESPONDER'S REFLECTION: You can't change the world until you set your mind on the things of God. Setting your mind on the things of God is all about focusing on what is important and not paying attention to those things that are not.

JANUARY 27TH

Psalm 130:1 —"Out of the depths I cry to you, Lord."

"Can you hear me now?" This phrase was a very popular slogan for a well-known cell phone company. Regardless of the phone carrier, you don't have to own a cell phone very long before you start to realize there can be problems. Why? Because phones are created by people and people are not perfect. However, God is perfect and he hears all the prayers you are praying. Friend, if it seems like God is taking a long time to answer your prayers, don't give up. Regardless of where you are at, keep sending those prayers up to God because he can hear you! Not only does God listen to our prayers, but oftentimes, he is moving mightily on our behalf without us even realizing it!

RESPONDER'S REFLECTION: You could be one prayer away from a miracle. Keep standing in faith, speaking in faith, and praying in faith!

JANUARY 28TH

Romans 5:8 —"But God demonstrates his own love for us in this: While we were still sinners, Christ died for us."

If you only view God as a judge, dictator, or an overbearing king, you are misunderstanding the nature of our loving father! This inaccurate view of who God the father really is, has sadly driven many people into fear, guilt, hopelessness, depression, insecurity, and a complete disconnect from the heart of God. Therefore, it is vital to understand the true nature of God. Yes, God disciplines us, corrects us, and at times judges our actions. However, these actions all come from his heart of love toward us. He desires to guide our lives into his blessings. The love of God will do whatever it takes to get us where we need to go.

RESPONDER'S REFLECTION: The motivation for God correcting us is love. He wants us to experience abundant supernatural life.

JANUARY 29TH

1 Corinthians 10:1 — "For I do not want you to be ignorant."

Sometimes in life, we can miss the obvious! On the other hand, sometimes we choose to ignore the issues that we face and struggle with each day. Friend, when it comes to the important things in life, we can't sweep those matters under the rug and not expect to pay the consequences at some point down the line. What are you struggling with that you are tempted to ignore? I want to encourage you that if you need to make a change in some area of your life, don't wait for tomorrow…start TODAY!

RESPONDER'S REFLECTION: Don't put off making necessary changes in your life because tomorrow is not promised. When you face an obstacle, don't run from it, run to it!

JANUARY 30TH

Hebrews 8:12 — "For I will forgive their wickedness and will remember their sins no more."

Have you ever noticed that many times, we tend to forget what God remembers and then we remember what God forgets? If you keep recalling your failures, mistakes, and sins, you have missed it! God has chosen to forget those faults. What does God remember? He remembers what his son, Jesus, accomplished on the cross for you. God remembers how you have called upon him to be your Lord and Savior. God remembers his incredible love for you. Therefore, quit focusing on what God has forgotten and instead, think about what God is remembering!

RESPONDER'S REFLECTION: Too many times, we forget what God remembers, and we remember what God forgets.

JANUARY 31ST

Psalm 147:3 — "He heals the brokenhearted and binds up their wounds."

God wants to bring emotional, relational, and physical healing to this world. Oftentimes, God uses people to heal people. Do you know what God desires for our life? Simply, his design is for loved people to love people, found people to find people, freed people to free people, and healed people to help people. We can know we are in God's will for our lives when we are doing these things.

RESPONDER'S REFLECTION: The only way to keep God's blessing is to give it away. God blesses us to be a blessing!

FEBRUARY 1ST

Esther 4:14 — "And who knows but that you have come to your royal position for such a time as this?"

Nothing changes if nothing changes! Queen Esther was about to see her people destroyed. She decided to step out in faith. God honored Esther's bold faith and saved the lives of her people. Many people want God's blessing in their finances, but they don't want to change. Many people want God's blessing in their relationships, but they don't want to change. Because Ester stepped out in faith, her obedience to God saved many people. Don't let the devil keep you in a prison of fear. Today, step out in faith and trust God for his very best for your life!

RESPONDER'S REFLECTION: Nothing changes if nothing changes! If you are tempted to settle for anything less than God's best, don't! Take a bold step of faith to change or make changes in your life.

FEBRUARY 2ND

Psalm 62:1 — "Truly my soul finds rest in God."

Peace is so valuable, yet we can't buy it! Peace is so vital to our daily existence, yet so many do not have it! Why is this the case? The answer is because peace only comes from God. If you want to have the rest and peace God offers, you have to come to him on his terms. Friend, if you want the peace of God, you have to take these simple, yet challenging steps:

1. Give your concerns honestly to God.
2. Leave your cares with God.
3. Keep trusting God even if there seems to be a delay with him answering your prayers.

RESPONDER'S REFLECTION: Nothing in this world can replace the rest and peace of God.

FEBRUARY 3RD

Matthew 25:21— "Well done, good and faithful servant!"

When we stand before God, he will not ask us if we have been successful. No! When we stand before God, he will ask us if we have been faithful. Many times, we focus on success and neglect faithfulness. Are you being faithful to meet with God daily in prayer and Bible reading? Have you been faithful to daily share the love of Jesus with others? Are you faithfully helping people who can't pay you back? Friend, the key to truly having a supernatural, abundant life is not found in seeking success; it is found in being faithful to God and his call on your life.

RESPONDER'S REFLECTION: When we stand before God, he will not ask us if we have been successful. When we stand before God, he will ask us if we have been faithful.

FEBRUARY 4TH

1 Corinthians 15:57 — "But thanks be to God!"

Sometimes during my prayer time, I spend a lot of time asking God for things. However, I am trying to change the way I spend that time with God. Before I ask God for anything, my goal is to make sure I first thank him for who he is and all he has given to me. Something powerful occurs when we share our grateful list with God before we take him our list of requests!

RESPONDER'S REFLECTION: It is very difficult for the enemy to defeat us when we are grateful to God. However, it is very easy for the enemy to defeat us when we live a life of complaining.

FEBRUARY 5TH

James 4:2-3 — "You do not have because you do not ask God. When you ask, you do not receive, because you ask with wrong motives..."

Prayer is powerful! However, if we pray for God to give us more money, but then refuse to work, that prayer has an increased likelihood of being unanswered! Prayer changes situations and prayer changes us. However, I believe there is a time when we must put legs to our prayers, which simply means putting action behind what you say you believe. Therefore, when you lay your requests before God keep praying and believing, but remember to start putting some legs on those prayers!

RESPONDER'S REFLECTION: Prayer changes things and prayer changes us! What are you doing to position yourself for God's blessings?

FEBRUARY 6TH

Joshua 1:5 — "I will never leave you nor forsake you."

God says he will never leave us. That verse means that even if sickness, sins, failures, pains, divorce, addictions, arrests, trials, or anything else that might happen to us, God promises not to leave us. Friend, you can have confidence knowing that God won't leave you no matter what might come against you. Isn't that good news?

RESPONDER'S REFLECTION: If you feel like God has left you, don't believe this lie. Our feelings aren't the truth. The Bible is the truth. What part of *never* do you not understand?

FEBRUARY 7TH

Genesis 1:1 — "In the beginning God created the heavens and the earth."

Are you facing problems in your life that seem insurmountable? Friend, if God created the heavens and the earth, he can certainly create an answer to any trouble you are encountering today. Even if you can't see an answer, trust that God is able to make a way. God is not limited by our power or understanding. Don't focus on what you can't do; focus on what God can do! Remember that he created the heavens and the earth and nothing is impossible for him.

RESPONDER'S REFLECTION: Don't focus on what you can't do; focus on what God can do! You can't be focusing on God and complaining at the same time.

FEBRUARY 8TH

Romans 1:17 — "The righteous will live by faith."

What you believe about God will determine how much of his blessings you have in your life! If you believe that God is a judge who is just waiting for any chance to come down on you, you won't have much of his blessing in your life. However, if you believe that God unconditionally loves you and wants to pour out his favor on your life, then you will receive an overflow of his blessings. The truth is that God wants your life full and overflowing with his goodness.

RESPONDER'S REFLECTION: What you believe about God will determine how much of his blessings you will have in your life.

FEBRUARY 9TH

Romans 8:31 — "If God is for us, who can be against us?"

Sometimes, we can all relate to the phrase - when it rains it pours! There have been moments in my life where I just thought everyone was against me. Many times, that kind of negative thought is just a lie from the devil. However, the truth is that even when it seems like everyone is against you, God is for you! Consider this good news that the Creator of the universe is on your side. Don't focus on who is against you, but instead focus on who is for you. God created you to be an overcomer!

RESPONDER'S REFLECTION: Don't focus on who is against you; focus on who is for you!

FEBRUARY 10TH

Jeremiah 16:20 —"Do people make their own gods? Yes, but they are not gods!"

At times, we have all been guilty of making a "god" in our life such as power, money, other people's approval, or anything else that takes our eyes off God. The problem is those "gods" are powerless over what really matters in life! Only Jesus has the power to forgive sins, heal lives, reconcile broken relationships, and bring what is dead back to life again. Today, make sure your focus is on the God who made you and not on the "god" you made. Anything we value more than the Lord is an idol.

RESPONDER'S REFLECTION: Are there other gods in your life? Make sure your focus is on the God who made you and not on the "god" you made!

FEBRUARY 11TH

2 Corinthians 10:5 —"We take captive every thought to make it obedient to Christ."

Have you ever had discouraging thoughts come to your mind such as "You can't do it" or "Remember that big mistake you made in the past"? At times, we can all struggle with these kinds of thoughts. How do we take every thought captive? Simply, feed the positive thoughts with God's Word, and starve the negative ones. If you starve the negative, hurtful thoughts that come to your mind, they will eventually leave. There is a simple principle we can apply to our lives: What you feed will grow and what you starve will die.

RESPONDER'S REFLECTION: It is easy to feed fear and doubt. Instead, feed your faith and doubt your doubts.

FEBRUARY 12TH

2 Corinthians 5:7 — "For we live by faith, not by sight."

Do you want God's favor to surround your life in a mighty way? If the answer is *yes,* then you will need to break out of your comfort zone. In reality, your comfort zone is a prison cell that will keep you confined to average, not taking risks and just scraping by with enough. However, God wants to bless you in abundance! In order to receive God's abundant blessing and favor, you must step out in faith. Today, live by faith and trust God to make your dreams come true.

RESPONDER'S REFLECTION: Comfort zones are prison cells for dreams. Don't let your dreams, visions, and desires be imprisoned.

FEBRUARY 13TH

Isaiah 2:22 — "Stop trusting in mere humans."

One of the biggest mistakes we can make is putting our hope in the created instead of the Creator. Doctors can heal a broken bone, but only God can heal a broken life. Counselors can listen to your problems, but only God can breathe life into a dead relationship. Nothing is impossible with God! Don't allow any person to sit on the throne of your life except for God. Put your trust in the Creator and watch how he will work in your life!

RESPONDER'S REFLECTION: God can do in one second what a thousand hours of human effort cannot. In your life, keep the main thing the main thing.

FEBRUARY 14TH

Matthew 11:28 — "Come to me, all you who are weary and burdened, and I will give you rest."

When we allow God to play a larger role in our lives, our problems start to become smaller. In contrast, when we only let God play a smaller role in our lives, our problems tend to grow larger. The bottom line is that you can't do life on your own and expect to have an abundant life. Today, invite God into your problems and messes and he will give you rest.

RESPONDER'S REFLECTION: God would like to make a crazy trade with you where you exchange your problems for his peace. Despite this amazing offer, so many people decide not to take God up on this tradeoff. Take God's deal today.

FEBRUARY 15TH

Joshua 24:15 — "But as for me and my household, we will serve the Lord."

One of the quickest ways to upset other people is to get involved in their business without being invited. If you want to repel others and not have many friends, then become nosey. Friend, sometimes the wisest thing we can do is mind our own business! Too many times, we are worried about other people's issues at the expense of neglecting to work on our own issues. Joshua 24:15 says, "But as for me and my household, we will serve the Lord." The devil will attempt to get us focused on other people's homes while ours could be crumbling down.

RESPONDER'S REFLECTION: We cannot live other people's lives. We can only live our life! Focus on making your life and your home a place where the presence of God is welcome.

FEBRUARY 16TH

Psalm 118:24 — "The Lord has done it this very day; let us rejoice today and be glad."

Do you know what the greatest day of your life is? It is TODAY! Why? Because today is the only day you can control. The decisions of the past are already decided and can't change. The choices of the future are still yet to be determined. However, we have this very day. Make the most out of today. Squeeze every bit of life out of today. Don't focus on the past or obsess about the future; focus on today. Today is your greatest day. Live life full throttle.

RESPONDER'S REFLECTION: Today is your greatest day! Do not let the devil steal it from you. The devil would love nothing more than for you to forfeit God's blessings today because of something in the past. Make the most of your life right now!

FEBRUARY 17TH

Philippians 1:6 — "Being confident of this, that he who began a good work in you will carry it on to completion until the day of Christ Jesus."

Don't get discouraged because God is not finished yet! Sometimes, we give up during the process of God working everything out in our job, relationships, or finances. Recently, I flew from Kansas City to Dallas and then finally to Little Rock, Arkansas. My first flight took me completely out of the way, but the flight wasn't finished and eventually I arrived to my intended final destination. So, as you are going through the process of life, just remember, "That he who began a good work in you will carry it on until completion."

RESPONDER'S REFLECTION: Sometimes God doesn't have us travel the shortest road to our dreams, but if we stay with him, he promises to get us there. Just keep being faithful to God.

FEBRUARY 18TH

Psalm 127:1 — "Unless the Lord builds the house, the builders labor in vain."

What are you building? Are you constructing your life around titles, money, or human accomplishments? If so, those achievements won't stand the test of time or eternity. However, if you allow God to use you to build up other people and his kingdom, those activities will produce an eternal reward. I once heard a pastor say, "Only one life will soon be past, and only what is done for Jesus will last."

RESPONDER'S REFLECTION: What are you building with your life today? You can either waste your life, spend your life, or invest your life. Invest your life into God and other people!

FEBRUARY 19TH

2 Corinthians 4:8 — "We are hard pressed on every side, but not crushed."

The great boxer Mike Tyson once said, "Everyone has a plan until they get punched in the face." Sometimes the idea of living for God can be exciting until life punches us in the face. Maybe today you are under a lot of stress and getting punched in the face by some aspect of life…hang in there! God promises that just because we face pressure in life, doesn't mean his purpose for our life is over. God has big dreams for your life if you just refuse to quit!

RESPONDER'S REFLECTION: You don't drown by falling into the water; you drown by staying in. If life punches you in the face, you can give life a gut punch by not quitting.

FEBRUARY 20TH

Matthew 1:21 — "You are to give him the name Jesus, because he will save his people from their sins."

Jesus came into this world to save people! He came to redeem people from sin and eternal death. Furthermore, he came to deliver and rescue people from guilt, pain, oppression, loneliness, anxiety, and fear. If you need God to save you from something, his answer is to call upon his one and only son, Jesus. However, God only saves those who want saving. Don't be too prideful to admit that you need help.

RESPONDER'S REFLECTION: God will only save those who want saving. At times, our own pride and arrogance can keep us from God's will, and then ultimately leave us broken. Be honest with God.

FEBRUARY 21ST

Isaiah 12:6 — "Shout aloud and sing for joy."

Joy is a choice! Sometimes it can be difficult to sing for joy or for that matter, do anything with joy. However, when we have difficulty living our lives in joy, oftentimes it is because we don't understand how to obtain joy. Simply stated, joy is a choice! Whether you realize it or not, each day when you wake up, you get an opportunity to choose joy or you can just choose to get by in life. Friend, I want to encourage you to choose joy today!

RESPONDER'S REFLECTION: Bitterness is a choice. Anger is a choice. Joy is a choice. What will you choose today?

FEBRUARY 22ND

Revelation 21:5 — "I am making everything new!"

Are you in a relationship that could use a new start? Is there a dream you have had for years that hasn't happened where a new beginning could help? There is good news — God has the supernatural power to make everything new! God doesn't just patch up the old or replace a few spark plugs; instead, he does a complete renovation to make things brand new. Get your hopes up for God to do something new in your life!

RESPONDER'S REFLECTION: God is not interested in just repairing the worn out, but he is interested in making the worn out new! God specializes in bringing new life to those things in our lives that are dead.

FEBRUARY 23RD

Psalm 23:6 — "Surely your goodness and love will follow me all the days of my life."

What an amazing promise! God wants his blessings to chase us down. Ponder on this verse, "Surely goodness and love will follow me." When you dwell on this thought for a moment, you realize how much God wants to pursue us with his love and blessings. When you are seeking after and submitting to God, his blessings will chase you down. No matter how fast you think you can run, you won't be able to outrun the blessings of God.

RESPONDER'S REFLECTION: Are you running from God or to God? Our plan often takes us away from God. God's plan always takes us to blessings.

FEBRUARY 24TH

Romans 2:1 —"For at whatever point you judge another, you are condemning yourself."

Would you consider making this year a judgment-free year? Many times, we judge others without having a clue as to what they have gone through. Mother Teresa once said, "If you judge people, you have no time to love them." The devil is trying to divide our marriages, homes, relationships, work places, and country. The weapon the enemy uses is judgment. When we allow ourselves to judge people, we start doing what God is supposed to do. All of us have hurts and issues. Leave the judging to God.

RESPONDER'S REFLECTION: Oftentimes, we judge others on what they do and we judge ourselves on our intentions. Be committed to making this a judgment-free year!

FEBRUARY 25TH

Matthew 6:19 —"Do not store up for yourselves treasures on earth, where moths and vermin destroy, and where thieves break in and steal."

The moment you were born, you began to die. None of us will get out of this life alive. What are you leaving behind? You can't leave a legacy if you don't have one. Have you dedicated your life to collecting stuff or touching the lives of other people? Friend, the accumulation of stuff is like a drug. The more things you acquire, the more you will need and it will never satisfy. Having money is acceptable as long as money doesn't have you. In order to be truly wealthy and to leave a rich legacy, you have to touch people with the love of Jesus. What type of legacy are you leaving?

RESPONDER'S REFLECTION: You can't leave a legacy if you don't have one. The only legacy a self-focused person leaves is a legacy no one wants. Focus on what is eternal.

FEBRUARY 26TH

Isaiah 25:1 — "For in perfect faithfulness you have done wonderful things."

Before my wife and I make any new purchases, we generally research the items online and read the reviews to ensure we are getting a good deal. However, we rarely find an item that has a perfect record or has always worked flawlessly. On the other hand, God's promises and love are perfectly faithful! Did you catch that truth? God's love and power are perfect, spotless, flawless, faultless, exact, inerrant, precise, and always just what we need! God knows what we need and he wants to give it to us.

RESPONDER'S REFLECTION: How God guides us is the correct and perfect way to go even if we don't feel like he is right. Just because you can't see God working doesn't mean he isn't.

FEBRUARY 27TH

Romans 6:14 — "You are not under the law, but under grace."

Many times, people don't understand what it means to be under God's grace! Let me explain:

Law is EARNED favor — If we obey the Ten Commandments 100% perfectly, we will be blessed and earn favor. This is old covenant living.

Grace is UNEARNED favor — Jesus obeyed the Ten Commandments 100% perfectly, yet paid the price for our sin with his life and blood. By believing in him, we receive favor. This is new covenant living.

Isn't it a blessing to get God's favor because of what Jesus did for us on the cross?

RESPONDER'S REFLECTION: You cannot earn grace. You don't achieve grace; you receive it!

FEBRUARY 28TH

Romans 15:13 — "So that you may overflow with hope."

What are you overflowing with today? If you bump a barrel full of water, what comes out of it? Obviously, the answer is water! If you are filled with worry, when the pressures of life bump you, inevitably worry comes out. If you are filled with anger, when the demands of life bump you, anger comes out. If you are filled with bitterness, and someone who treats you unfairly bumps you, bitterness comes out. Today, give God all the junk that is going on in your life so that the hope of God will fill you so full that it will overflow out of you!

RESPONDER'S REFLECTION: What you are full of will always come out. What are you filling your life with today?

FEBRUARY 29TH

2 Corinthians 10:17 — "Let the one who boasts boast in the Lord."

Don't be stuck in the rut of being negative all the time. It is easy to argue, whine, and complain about the difficulties of life. Friend, when you are negative all the time, I promise that you will have fewer friends. However, the main reason we shouldn't speak negatively is that we will start to believe what we are saying. Today, I want to encourage you to let the goodness of God filter what you say. Sure, you might have problems, but remember that God has an answer to any problem you might struggle with in your life.

RESPONDER'S REFLECTION: Instead of telling God how big your problems are, would you start telling your problems how big your God is?

MARCH 1ST

Matthew 9:24 — "He (Jesus) said, 'Go away. The girl is not dead but asleep.' But they laughed at him."

There are times when others may laugh at you for following God. In today's verse, we see that people were laughing at Jesus. His response to their scoffing was simply that he raised the dead girl back to life, and this miracle silenced the crowd. We can learn two factors from this verse: 1. Jesus always brings life to people, marriages, jobs, and you name it. 2. If others mock you for serving God, let the life of God flow out of you and soon those who were laughing may start to follow you!

RESPONDER'S REFLECTION: Don't let how other people respond to you affect your relationship with God. If you take a stand for Jesus, people will start to follow.

MARCH 2ND

Micah 7:19 — "You will again have compassion on us; you will tread our sins underfoot and hurl all our iniquities into the depths of the sea."

Not only does God give us his compassion today, but he also makes an amazing claim that he will hurl all of our sins and junk into the depths of the sea! Wow, praise God! However, the only problem is that sometimes we decide to break out our fishing poles and try to fish up what God has hurled into the sea. Friend, God has forgiven and healed you. Make sure you put up a "No Fishing" sign over your past failures because God has placed your mistakes under his feet.

RESPONDER'S REFLECTION: Your past is not a place of residence, but a point of reference. Stop remembering what God has forgotten.

MARCH 3RD

Philippians 4:13 —"I can do all this through him who gives me strength."

You are stronger than you think you are! Oh yes, you are! The Bible states that if you are in Christ you can do all things! However, sometimes we don't act and live as if we have the God-given power to do all things. Do not believe the lies of the devil today. The truth isn't based on how you feel or think. The truth is that you are stronger than you think you are!

RESPONDER'S REFLECTION: What limits have you allowed others or yourself to place on your life? Ask God to help you remove any of these barriers from your life. When our lives are lived without limits, we can start to experience abundant life! You are stronger than you think you are.

MARCH 4TH

Ephesians 1:19-20 —"That power is the same as the mighty strength he exerted when he raised Christ from the dead."

Oftentimes, we want the power of Jesus to heal, encourage, or change people's lives. However, one important principle we need to understand is that we can't have the power of Jesus without living like Jesus. If you want to have the power of Jesus in your life, you must love, serve, and care for people just as Jesus did. He is an amazing example to follow!

RESPONDER'S REFLECTION: Supernatural power flows into our lives when we stop living life our way and start living life God's way. If the power of Jesus isn't alive in you, something is wrong.

MARCH 5TH

Romans 10:13 —"Everyone who calls on the name of the Lord will be saved."

Christians need to start realizing that it is about time we start working together! Unfortunately, we have allowed denominational church lines to divide us for far too many years. We need to put an end to this division! The devil is badly attacking our world and he is doing so through an age-old military concept, divide and conquer. Today, I want to challenge you to become an ACTS Christian:

A = All
C = Christians
T = Together
S = Serving

RESPONDER'S REFLECTION: We are stronger together. Don't let the devil keep you away from other Christians simply because there is a different sign over their church entrance.

MARCH 6TH

John 13:34 —"A new command I give you: Love one another."

God commands us to love our spouses, honor our parents, and to love one another. However, sometimes our relationships can go sideways. There is one key concept that can help you when it comes to relationships, and that is, my response is my responsibility! Your spouse or friend can't make you respond in a hurtful or ungodly way. You control how *you* will respond. If you truly want healthy relationships, you need to respond to others in love even when you don't feel like it and even when they don't deserve it!

RESPONDER'S REFLECTION: My response is my responsibility. You can't control others but you can control you.

MARCH 7TH

Matthew 7:7 — "Ask and it will be given to you."

Friend, God wants to answer your prayers! However, you can't ask small and receive big. If you ask small, you will receive small. If you ask little, you will receive little. However, the opposite is true as well. If you ask big, you will receive big. If you ask large, you will receive large. Therefore, the important question for you to answer is how big is your ask? Have you been praying too small?

RESPONDER'S REFLECTION: You can't ask small and receive big. How big is your ask? Begin to ask God big!

MARCH 8TH

Philippians 2:14 — "Do everything without grumbling or arguing."

The more we complain, the weaker we become. Conversely, the more grateful we are, the stronger we become. At its very core, complaining can be so destructive whereas, gratefulness is so life giving. Many of us have overwhelming blessings standing right in front of us, yet we miss them when we are not thankful. When we spend time around someone who is grateful, it is attractive and contagious. On the other hand, when we hang out with someone who is a chronic complainer, it is repellant. Today, spend less time complaining and more time being grateful!

RESPONDER'S REFLECTION: The more you complain the weaker you become; whereas, the more grateful you are, the stronger you become.

MARCH 9TH

Romans 8:1 —"Therefore, there is now no condemnation for those who are in Christ Jesus."

Guilt stinks! We can't put toothpaste back in its tube. But, if we turn to God and ask for forgiveness when we sin or drop the ball, he alone removes the guilt of our sin and takes us off the hook. Notice the important word in today's verse, "now." When we go to God, he forgives *now.* You don't want to go through life feeling guilty all the time. Best of all, God doesn't want you to walk in shame either. Today, if you are feeling guilty about a past mistake, take it to God and grasp the truth that there is *now* no condemnation!

RESPONDER'S REFLECTION: God wants you free from any shame or guilt you are dealing with today. The devil wants you in bondage and God wants you free!

MARCH 10TH

Proverbs 17:28 —"Even fools are thought wise if they keep silent."

When we say something we regret, it is impossible to take those words back. You can't unscramble eggs. Friend, we can learn a serious amount of wisdom when we keep our mouth shut while we go through the tough issues of life. You can always go back and add something to a conversation if you need to later, but you can never take away words you misspoke. Practice listening more and you will see an extra measure of God's blessing in your life!

RESPONDER'S REFLECTION: God has given you two ears and one mouth, which means you are supposed to listen twice as much as you talk.

MARCH 11TH

Psalm 37:39 — "The salvation of the righteous comes from the Lord; he is their stronghold in time of trouble."

When life gets crazy, sometimes we can become desperate and turn to the wrong answers. For example, when we fight with our spouses, we might resort to yelling. When we battle stress, we might turn to substances or overindulge on foods that aren't healthy for us. There are numerous other examples besides these. Today, I want to encourage you that God is your stronghold. The key to victory in our lives is to turn to God at all times, but especially to do so when our flesh is trying to resist and wants to turn to unhealthy options. God loves you and he is your stronghold!

RESPONDER'S REFLECTION: Hell and every demon who resides there can't stop a man or woman who is empowered by God. You are unstoppable when you are serving Jesus!

MARCH 12TH

Proverbs 20:22 — "Do not say, 'I'll pay you back for this wrong!' Wait for the Lord, and he will avenge you."

Are you fighting with someone? Has that person betrayed you? The worst thing you can do is retaliate by fighting back and taking matters into your own hands. The better way to handle any opposition is to wait for God and allow him to take care of the situation on your behalf. Oftentimes when we try to do all the fighting on our own, we actually end up making things worse!

RESPONDER'S REFLECTION: If you fight fire with fire, everyone ends up getting burned. Instead of fighting fire with fire, fight fire with faith! Faith is a powerful weapon that is deeply underused today.

MARCH 13TH

Proverbs 21:11—"When a mocker is punished, the simple gain wisdom; by paying attention to the wise they get knowledge."

Are you acquainted with a "know-it-all"? As soon as you read that question, a face or name might have popped into your mind. Sometimes, if we are honest, we have all acted like a know-it-all. By that statement, I mean that we aren't always teachable when someone else tries to impart us with wisdom or knowledge. Can I share one of my favorite phrases with you? Wisdom is learning from other people's mistakes. The wise person sees another person's errors and changes course. The smart person sees another person's failings and changes direction. We can't have God's blessing and be know-it-alls.

RESPONDER'S REFLECTION: Wisdom is learning from other people's mistakes.

MARCH 14TH

2 Peter 1:4 —"He has given us his very great and precious promises."

Don't give up on God's promises! Oftentimes, we have to wait for the promises of God to come to fruition. However, take a moment to consider that some of the greatest gifts in life have a wait time! A mother must wait nine months before her baby is born. A college student attends school for typically four years before graduation. Jesus, himself, had a three-day wait time before he rose from the grave! Friend, if Jesus had a wait time, so will we. Don't give up on God's promises for your life!

RESPONDER'S REFLECTION: The greatest promises in life will have a wait time. Don't give in to impatience!

MARCH 15TH

Proverbs 27:2 — "Let someone else praise you, and not your own mouth."

When you hear people sing their own praises, it is actually an outward sign of an inward problem. Here are the internal issues associated with praising oneself:

1. Pride
2. Insecurity
3. Lack of ability to connect with others in a genuine way
4. Dependency on oneself instead of on God

At one time or another, we have all been guilty of bragging about ourselves. But, I want to encourage you to live a life that pleases God and then let God promote you when the time is right!

RESPONDER'S REFLECTION: Pride has taken down some of the greatest leaders in public service, ministry, and military service. Let God lift you up.

MARCH 16TH

John 14:12 — "Very truly I tell you, whoever believes in me will do the works I have been doing, and they will do even greater things than these."

Wow! Did you read that verse? God wants to do more in your life than you ever thought was possible. In addition, Jesus says, "They will do even greater things than these." When you place your faith in Jesus, you not only have the power to do what Jesus did, but he also says that you will do even greater things! We serve an amazing God! Today, believe him to do the impossible in your life!

RESPONDER'S REFLECTION: Today, place your faith in God to do those things you don't believe you can do.

MARCH 17TH

Philippians 2:5 —"Have the same mindset as Christ Jesus"

In order to have the power of Jesus you must have the attitude of Jesus! You can't change the world till you change your attitude. Our mindset and attitude determine so much in our lives. Don't let your attitude become your prison. The mindset of the world says you have limitations but the mindset of Jesus says all things are possible. The mindset of the world says you are defeated but the mindset of Jesus says you are a champion. The mindset of the world says you are weak but the mindset of Jesus says you can do all things. Which attitude will you give into today? The majority of people you are around have given into the mindset of the world, be different! Jesus has given you all the power you need to have victory in life!

RESPONDER'S REFLECTION: In order to have the power of Jesus you have to have the attitude of Jesus. Don't let your attitude become your prison. You can't change the world till you change your attitude!

MARCH 18TH

Isaiah 51:10 —"Was it not you who dried up the sea, the waters of the great deep, who made a road in the depths of the sea so that the redeemed might cross over?"

In this Bible story, God's people were surrounded. The people of God had enemies advancing behind them and a large body of water in front of them. They were trapped, and it seemed like they had no way out. But God made a way! Today, you might feel hemmed in by some serious issues concerning your health, marriage, finances, or life where you believe there is no escape. However, don't believe that lie from the devil because God can make a way out of any impossible or painful situation you might be facing.

RESPONDER'S REFLECTION: If God brings you to it, he will bring you through it! No matter what the roadblock is God has a way around it, over it, or through it.

MARCH 19TH

Matthew 6:33 — "But seek first his kingdom and his righteousness."

Have you ever noticed how much our culture has changed over the years? It used to be an acceptable concept by most people that in a job (or anything) a person needed to start at the bottom and work their way up. In this day, people would rather just start at the top. In God's kingdom, we have to start at the beginning. We don't get to start at the finish line. However, if we are faithful, God will advance and bless us. Today, I want to encourage you not to get discouraged if you have to start at the bottom. Just remember to put God first and everything else will work out.

RESPONDER'S REFLECTION: God blesses faithfulness. The more faithful you are, the more blessed you will become! Seek God first!

MARCH 20TH

2 Corinthians 5:17 — "Therefore, if anyone is in Christ, the new creation has come: The old has gone, the new is here!"

Wouldn't it be nice to get a fresh start in a relationship? Can you imagine getting another chance to make that vision a reality? How amazing would it be to get another shot at receiving your dream job? Friend, the good news is God is a God of second, third, fourth, and eighty-seventh chances. If you go to God, he will give you a fresh start and will turn the situations you are encountering into new opportunities!

RESPONDER'S REFLECTION: Jesus is a healing, loving, miracle working Savior. However, what Jesus is not — he is not done with you yet!

MARCH 21ST

2 Corinthians 1:24 — "It is by faith you stand firm."

God intends for you to have his power, blessings, and wisdom! However, you can't feed your fears and then expect to have God's very best for your life. Friend, every one of us has a choice we need to make each day. Will we walk in fear or in faith? We can talk in fear or talk in faith. We can think in fear or think in faith. Today, stand firm and trust God!

RESPONDER'S REFLECTION: You can't feed your fears and expect to have God's best for your life. Stand firm and don't let anyone move you off what God wants you to do.

MARCH 22ND

2 Corinthians 6:18 — "'I will be a Father to you, and you will be my sons and daughters,' says the Lord Almighty."

What an incredible deal that the Creator of the universe wants to be our Father. Consider the notion that God eagerly desires to adopt you and to have a personal relationship with you. God isn't offering to be your religious leader or spiritual trainer. God is offering and desiring to be your Father! Today, would you allow God to lead, heal, and guide you as a loving dad?

RESPONDER'S REFLECTION: If you want to bless God, simply spend time with him.

MARCH 23RD

Jeremiah 29:11 — "For I know the plans I have for you."

Today's scripture is valuable because God has personalized this promise just for you! God did not say, "For I know the plans I have for the *world.*" No! God said, "For I know the plans I have for *you.*" Friend, God has incredible miracle-working plans just for *you!* So, if you are tempted to believe that your best days are behind you or that you don't have an exciting future ahead of you, please don't believe this lie. God loves you deeply and he has great plans just for you!

RESPONDER'S REFLECTION: Your best days are ahead of you. If you don't believe this truth, you are missing what God is trying to say to you.

MARCH 24TH

Psalm 121:3 — "He will not let your foot slip."

What problems or issues are you dealing with today? From time to time, we all struggle with the worries of this world. However, the good news is that as long as you aren't quitting, you are making progress. This old cliché is so true in that "What doesn't kill you makes you stronger." Today, give God the trials you are dealing with and he makes an amazing promise that, "He will not let your foot slip." Don't give up, don't give in, and don't stop pressing forward! As long as you don't quit, you are making progress.

RESPONDER'S REFLECTION: You can only fail if you quit.

MARCH 25TH

2 Timothy 1:7 — "For the Spirit God gave us does not make us timid."

One of the devil's greatest attacks on our lives is fear. The majority of the time we fear something that may never happen. What exactly is fear?

F = False
E = Evidence
A = Appearing
R = Real

Today, as you go through the adventure of life, do not give into fear! God has created you to be powerful! I once heard a preacher say, "You can be pitiful, or you can be powerful, but you can't be both." Which will you choose today?

RESPONDER'S REFLECTION: Most of the time, what we fear never happens.

MARCH 26TH

Proverbs 21:21 — "Whoever pursues righteousness and love finds life, prosperity and honor."

What are you pursuing? Are you chasing after wealth? Are you trying to make a name for yourself? Are you trying to get ahead? When we pursue wealth, position, or power, those things can wreck our lives if we are not careful. It isn't necessarily bad to have those things, but if they become our focus, it can be our undoing! Friend, when we pursue God and righteousness, the natural byproduct is his blessing. Today, I want to encourage you to chase after God above all, and then everything else will line up!

RESPONDER'S REFLECTION: Pursuing God and his righteousness means that you always put God first in your life.

MARCH 27TH

Isaiah 48:22 — "'There is no peace,' says the Lord, 'for the wicked.'"

How do people mess up their lives? The answer is that they embrace the evil and immorality that God is against for their lives. Some of the more obvious signs of wickedness that is not pleasing to God are easy to detect such as murder, adultery, stealing, and the like. However, sometimes we all struggle with sin that isn't as noticeable at first glance. For example, jealousy, envy, unforgiveness, and slander can many times fly under the radar. Today, I want to encourage you to do a soul-search, let go of anything in your life that God is against, and embrace what God is for!

RESPONDER'S REFLECTION: What we entertain will control us. In order to live life to the fullest, we need to make sure that our lives, on the inside and out, turn away from evil. We cannot entertain evil and live a blessed life.

MARCH 28TH

Proverbs 25:19 — "Like a broken tooth or a lame foot is reliance on the unfaithful in a time of trouble."

Do you want to become the best employee at your workplace? Would you like to bless the socks off your spouse? Would you like to be the person others enjoy being around? If so, then simply be faithful in all that you do. Being faithful does not mean you will be perfect or all knowing, but it means you will be steadfast, loyal, and dependable. Sadly, faithfulness is a basic principle that seems uncommon in our society today. Today, resolve to be faithful in what you do and in what others ask of you, and you will encounter great success and significance.

RESPONDER'S REFLECTION: One notable way you demonstrate that you are faithful is when other people know they can count on you. People are looking for others who are dependable.

MARCH 29TH

Hebrews 10:39 —"But we do not belong to those who shrink back and are destroyed, but to those who have faith and are saved."

Don't run *from* your problems, run *to* them! None of us is fast enough to flee from our troubles. However, if we run to our problems and face them in the strength and power of God, we will overcome them. Even if all hell is breaking loose, when we believe and put our faith in God, he promises to save us! Stop running from the issues and trials you are facing today.

RESPONDER'S REFLECTION: What are you running from? Step out in faith and lean into that issue. It doesn't take courage to ignore the problems we face. It does take a hero's courage to face what we don't want to face.

MARCH 30TH

Ephesians 5:16—"Making the most of every opportunity."

Today, you have the opportunity to:

1. Focus on the positives in your life
2. Encourage others
3. Show your family how much you love them
4. Try something new
5. Believe God for something greater in your life

Don't waste today! Make the most of the opportunities God gives you each day.

RESPONDER'S REFLECTION: What is something you would like to do but haven't begun yet? Start it today!

MARCH 31ST

2 Corinthians 1:3-4—"The God of all comfort, who comforts us in all our troubles, so that we can comfort those in any trouble with the comfort we ourselves receive from God."

Did you notice the two powerful points in these verses? First, God can comfort us through any troubles we face. Secondly, we are to let him use us to comfort others. Friend, if you need comfort, don't believe the lie that what you are going through is too much or too big. Secondly, throughout today, let God use you to bring healing to other people's lives.

RESPONDER'S REFLECTION: God uses people to heal people. Whom are you going to partner with God to help heal today? You may be the answer to someone's prayer.

APRIL 1ST

Philippians 4:13 —"I can do all this."

Yes, you can! However, the devil will always lie and tell you that you can't. He will try to convince you that you can't overcome an issue, you can't accomplish a task, or he might even whisper in your ear that you can't make a comeback. However, don't listen to the devil because he doesn't have the last word. Instead, heed what God says because he does have the final word. And God is saying yes, you can! Friend, we can accomplish all things because we have access to God's power through Jesus. Today, receive this great news that yes, you can!

RESPONDER'S REFLECTION: The devil will always try to tell you that you can't be blessed, you can't have God's favor, and you can't accomplish amazing things. In contrast, God wants you to hear that yes, you can!

APRIL 2ND

John 14:1 —"Do not let your hearts be troubled."

Occasionally, we all face trials and go through times of discouragement. When we grow disheartened, we are supposed to go *through* discouragement, but not *live* in discouragement. Consider these three truths about God that will hopefully encourage you to move past the disappointments you may be encountering:

1. No matter what you are facing today, God has an answer.
2. God can heal and turn around any pain you encounter to use as a blessing.
3. You might feel alone but you are never alone because God is with you.

RESPONDER'S REFLECTION: We are supposed to go *through* discouragement, not *live* in discouragement.

APRIL 3RD

Isaiah 57:13—"But whoever takes refuge in me will inherit the land."

What a powerful thought! When we choose to make God our refuge above anything else, we will receive his victory. We are all taking refuge in something or someone. We need to avoid the trap of only seeking after the blessings instead of pursuing the One who gives the blessings. When we simply seek God and make him our refuge, his supernatural power will then be displayed in our life.

RESPONDER'S REFLECTION: Don't fall into the trap of seeking the blessing over the One who gives the blessing. Remember to always seek and take refuge in God alone.

APRIL 4TH

2 Corinthians 6:2 —"I tell you, now is the time of God's favor, now is the day of salvation."

God's Word is very clear, "Now is the time." Therefore, now is the time to:

1. Start living your dreams
2. Make a bold move
3. Forgive others even if they haven't asked for your forgiveness
4. Step out in faith
5. Believe God for his outrageous promises for your life

Most people wait to start living! Today, make a decision that you are going to be a *now* person.

RESPONDER'S REFLECTION: Don't wait to start living the abundant life God wants you to have!

APRIL 5TH

James 4:7 —"Submit yourselves, then, to God. Resist the devil, and he will flee from you."

Have you ever tried to stop doing something that was difficult for you to give up? Sometimes, we develop habits. However, the bad news is that if we form a habit, soon the habit starts to form us. What is the answer? Some people believe that we must resist the devil, which is partially true. However, the first step to breaking habits, addictions, and walking in God's power is to submit to God. Yielding to God is the gateway to supernatural power. Therefore, submit your plans, hurts, and dreams to God today.

RESPONDER'S REFLECTION: If we form a habit, soon the habit starts to form us. What habits are you forming that you need to quit?

APRIL 6TH

Colossians 3:2 — "Set your minds on things above, not on earthly things."

Oftentimes, the greatest battle we face is in our minds. When we worry about earthly things, our minds become distracted and not focused on the things of God. Friend, I want to encourage you today to set your mind on gratefulness, righteousness, and on God's love. It is so easy to allow this world to get our minds preoccupied and set on the wrong things. You can choose where you will set your mind, so keep it focused on God!

RESPONDER'S REFLCTION: Nobody can control your thinking but you. If you want to live an abundant life, you must get rid of mediocre thinking. You can't change your life until you change your thinking.

APRIL 7TH

Matthew 5:44 — "But I tell you, love your enemies and pray for those who persecute you."

Throughout scripture, God teaches us to do the opposite of what our flesh would desire. For example, in Matthew 20:16, we read that the first shall be last. In Acts 20:35, we learn that it is better to give than to receive. The Bible also instructs us that in order to live for God, we need to die to our fleshly desires. These are all examples where God shares with us to do the opposite of what we want to do. So if someone is opposing or persecuting you, give them the love of God. Watch what God will do when you abandon your ways to follow his.

RESPONDER'S REFLECTION: Loving your enemies will go so much further in restoring your relational issues than fighting fire with fire.

APRIL 8TH

Psalm 23:4 — "Even though I walk through the darkest valley, I will fear no evil, for you are with me."

Oftentimes, when people read this verse they mainly focus on the part where God says he will be with us through our darkest times. No doubt, this truth is awesome news! However, I also want you to see another important word in this verse, *walk*. I don't know about you, but I want to *run* through the dark times and get to the good times as quickly as possible. Yet, God does not work in this way! We have to walk through the difficult times so we can learn from pain, appreciate blessings, and have a testimony to share with others. If you are walking through some tough things today, just remember God has a purpose and plan for the pain you endure.

RESPONDER'S REFLECTION: Your setback can become a setup for a comeback if you will learn from it.

APRIL 9TH

Romans 8:28 — "And we know that in all things God works for the good of those who love him."

I have the blessing to travel all over the place and share the good news of God's love. However, many times when I fly, I have to take a connecting flight that takes me to another state completely out of the way before I finally arrive to my final destination. Sometimes, God does the same thing with us. He has a plan to get us to a certain destination, but he may lead us completely out of the way before we actually reach the end of our journey. We may think we are going in the wrong direction, but in reality, God is leading us on the path to our blessing. Friend, maybe you feel like your life is going in the wrong direction. Just remember that God rarely puts us on a direct non-stop flight to our blessing. Most of the time God puts us on a connecting flight to get us to our ultimate destination.

RESPONDER'S REFLECTION: God wants to use every part of the journey to bless us.

APRIL 10TH

Proverbs 18:21 — "The tongue has the power of life and death."

This scripture is so powerful! The only two ways you can use your words today is either to build others up or tear them down. Truly, those are the only options you have! Sadly, we have all experienced other people using their hurtful words to bring pain into our lives. When you are tempted to speak unkind words about others, remember that every person you meet today is created in the image of God. As easy as it can be to tear people down, make a decision to use your words to encourage and build others up and you will change your world and theirs!

RESPONDER'S REFLECTION: My first Police Chief, Fred Mills, used to say, "We treat suspects like ladies and gentlemen not because they are, but because we are." These are wise words in how we should treat other people we disagree with.

APRIL 11TH

Ephesians 1:19-20 — "And his incomparably great power for us who believe. That power is the same as the mighty strength he exerted when he raised Christ from the dead."

You are more powerful than you think you are! Yes, you read this statement correctly. You are more powerful than you think you are! Once you put your faith in God, you are partnering with the supernatural, miracle working, Creator of the universe. The problems you are concerned about today are so small compared to the power of God at work within you. However, the reality is that our small problems seem large to us. Yet God has given you his power to destroy every roadblock and have his blessing in your life. Put your faith in God today and recognize that you are more powerful than you think you are!

RESPONDER'S REFLECTION: Don't miss your moment. The power your need to have victory in this life does not come from you and it never will. The only place to receive supernatural power is in God.

APRIL 12TH

Mark 16:6 — "You are looking for Jesus the Nazarene, who was crucified. He has risen!"

Have the trials and hardships of life knocked you down? Friend, can I give you a word from God? Get up! If David defeated Goliath, if Daniel survived the lion's den, and if Jesus rose from the grave, than you can overcome any problem you are facing. Jesus rose from the dead and through that miracle, he graciously gives us his power to get up when we are down.

RESPONDER'S REFLECTION: You don't drown by falling into the water; you drown by staying in it. If life has knocked you down, Jesus is giving you the power to get back up. Get up today and defeat what has been attacking you!

APRIL 13TH

1 John 3:1 — "See what great love the Father has lavished on us, that we should be called children of God! And that is what we are!"

As you read this verse, I want you to consider two thoughts:

1. Your daddy determines your destiny. Once you put your faith in Jesus Christ, you are now a child of God. God's destiny and plans for you are so much bigger once you submit your own vision to God's vision instead.
2. Your papa determines your purpose. God has a supernatural plan and purpose for your life. If you want your life to count and make a difference, draw closer to God. The closer you are to God, the more his purpose flows into your life.

RESPONDER'S REFLECTION: Your identity and power doesn't come from who you are, but instead, it comes from *whose* you are.

APRIL 14TH

Hebrews 2:18 — "He is able to help those who are being tempted."

What is enticing you today? At times, we all struggle with temptation and sometimes we give in to that temptation. First, we need to realize that we can't overcome temptation on our own. We need Jesus and other believers for accountability. Oftentimes, God uses people to heal other people. Secondly, when you give into temptation, it is important to overcome the next battle, which is the thought of giving up. Be encouraged that you can overcome any temptation or struggle you face today. Don't buy into one of the devil's greatest temptations, which is the temptation to give up!

RESPONDER'S REFLECTION: One of the greatest temptations we will ever face is the temptation to give up. Don't do it!

APRIL 15TH

Hebrews 3:1 — "Fix your thoughts on Jesus."

It is so easy to get worried! Just turning on the news can get you so discouraged! God has an answer to the mental battles you might be facing. Fix your thoughts on Jesus when:

1. Your marriage starts to go sideways.
2. You have problems with your job or career.
3. You have too much month at the end of the money.
4. You don't know what to do.

The bottom line is that you need to fix your thoughts on Jesus. Are you starting to get the message?

RESPONDER'S REFLECTION: Whatever stage of life you're in today, fix your eyes on Jesus.

APRIL 16TH

Romans 5:8 —"But God demonstrates his own love for us."

Before this day is over, 117 people will have sadly committed suicide. Every year, almost twice as many people commit suicide compared to those killed by homicide. Ultimately, people listen to and become deceived by the lies the devil tells them. Can I give you a few examples of those lies?

1. You are a failure.
2. You have made too many mistakes.
3. You can never recover what you have lost.
4. You won't ever be able to overcome that addiction.

These statements are all inaccurate and false! The truth is God loves you and you can defeat any obstacle you are facing today.

RESPONDER'S REFLECTION: Committing suicide is a permanent solution to a temporary problem.

APRIL 17TH

Psalm 136:1 —"Give thanks to the Lord, for he is good."

Everything you deem as good in your life comes from God. Everyone who is a blessing in your life is a gift from God. Every breath you take in this life is a present from God. William Arthur Ward said it best, "Feeling gratitude and not expressing it is like wrapping a present and not giving it." Make sure you are thanking God for all the good things you have in your life. Thankfulness in one's life is often a measuring device for maturity.

RESPONDER'S REFLECTION: The more grateful we are, the more stable and powerful we become. The more we complain, the more inconsistent and weaker we become.

APRIL 18TH

Matthew 7:1 —"Do not judge, or you too will be judged."

Friend, sometimes we confuse our job with God's. I have seen believers who function like umpires, where they think they should make the call on whether others are out or safe based on how they live their lives. In reality, God is the only one who can make the call. As believers, God doesn't ask us to be umpires, but lifeguards. We are supposed to dive in to rescue people and share with them the way of salvation through Jesus. Why don't we let God be the umpire and we will just focus on seeing lives transformed by the love of God!

RESPONDER'S REFLECTION: God doesn't call on us to be umpires, but lifeguards.

APRIL 19TH

Philippians 2:13 —"For it is God who works in you."

A while back, I believe God was trying to communicate a message to me. I was working diligently at the church I was serving at as an Associate Pastor, when suddenly, I felt like God told me to step out and start a new ministry called Serving Pastors. However, this past week, I believe God said to me, "Barry, stop working so hard *for* me!" Then, the second part of his message was, "Start working *with* me." Friend, I want to ask you this one question… Are you working *for* God or *with* God? We can accomplish so much more when we are working with God and not for him! Isn't that good news?

RESPONDER'S REFLECTION: Stop spending all your time working *for* God, and start spending your time working *with* God.

APRIL 20TH

Exodus 20:3 — "You shall have no other gods before me."

An idol is anything in your life that gets in between you and God. One of the many problems with making power, substances, money, or possessions our "god" is that those things are powerless to help us when we are facing the real problems of life. However, God is a God who answers his people when they cry out to him. Therefore, take the time to uncover and remove any idol from your life that would try to sneak in between you and God.

RESPONDER'S REFLECTION: We need to worship the Creator, not the created. Don't let anyone or anything come in between you and God.

APRIL 21ST

Isaiah 58:11 — "The Lord will guide you always."

If your dreams don't intimidate you, they aren't big enough! God rarely asks us to do things we can do in our own power. Friend, the Bible is full of stories about men and women who accomplished great things they couldn't do in their own strength. As you go through your day, realize that God can give you amazing dreams to fulfill because he is the one guiding you. God not only promises to direct your steps today, but he promises to guide you always!

RESPONDER'S REFLECTION: If God makes you a promise, you can take it to the bank. If your dreams don't intimidate you, they aren't big enough!

APRIL 22ND

Matthew 19:26 —"With God all things are possible."

The truth is that with God, there are no limits, but with man, there are limits. If you believe you will fail, you will. If you believe you will not make it, you won't. However, if you put your faith in God, no matter how big the obstacle, you can have victory. You have a choice today; you can trust what you only see in the natural, or you can trust what you know to be true from God's Word, which is supernatural. Just remember that with God, nothing is impossible!

RESPONDER'S REFLECTION: The key to victory in life is simply to answer this question: Will you believe your feelings or will you believe God?

APRIL 23RD

Proverbs 21:1 —"In the Lord's hand the king's heart is a stream of water that he channels toward all who please him."

No earthly power has intimidated God! It doesn't matter the amount of wealth, wisdom, or size of the army, God can handle anyone! He has total rule over everything, so that means he can handle your boss, your spouse, your co-worker, or even your enemy. God can and will give you the strength to handle any relationship issue. Why? Because any heart in the hand of God is like water. Allow God to use you to be a healing agent to all you meet.

RESPONDER'S REFLECTION: Don't view the obstacles you may face through your own eyes and power. Instead, view them through the eyes of God and his power.

APRIL 24TH

Jeremiah 31:25 — "I will refresh the weary and satisfy the faint."

Recently, my wife and I enjoyed a nice vacation to celebrate our anniversary. It was such a blessing to be alone with her for so many days! Even though our vacation was amazing, the trip ended and we are back in the real world. When it comes to God, he gives us rest and refreshment that far exceeds a thousand vacations. As great as vacations are, there is always a time limit with them. But with God's peace, there is no starting or ending point. Today, turn to God as your source of strength, wisdom, and peace.

RESPONDER'S REFLECTION: Our rest and peace in life can only be found in the loving arms of God.

APRIL 25TH

Isaiah 43:19 — "See, I am doing a new thing! Now it springs up; do you not perceive it?"

What new thing is God trying to do in your life that you are fighting him on? Even though your yesterday was possibly full of blessings, God wants to move and do something fresh in your life today! However, if we want to receive God's blessings for today, we need to be open about allowing the new something or someone into our life. For many of us, trying something new can be a hassle or even terrifying. But that hassle might be totally worth it because it could mean a new adventure into God's supernatural provision for your life.

RESPONDER'S REFLECTION: God wants to do something new in your life. Don't let the victories and blessings of yesterday keep you from victories and blessings for today.

APRIL 26TH

Matthew 9:29 — "According to your faith let it be done to you."

Do you believe that God can dramatically reverse any difficult situation in your life? Don't put your faith in man, or things created by man. Instead, place your faith in God because with him, all things are possible. Sometimes, we may have to wait or persevere in our faith, but if we will keep our faith in God, the negative issues in our lives will begin to change. Faith starts with nothing and ends with everything. Faith stands when everyone else sits. Faith boldly declares what will be, not what is. Your faith will determine the level of power you have in life.

RESPONDER'S REFLECTION: Faith in God can move mountains. Fear in life takes us from being an overcomer to being overcome.

APRIL 27TH

Proverbs 15:3 — "The eyes of the Lord are everywhere."

A fool says in his heart that there is no God. But greater is the fool who knows there is a God, yet lives like there isn't one. God is watching and observing today. Nothing gets past his eyes. When we do things privately to encourage and build others up, God notices our actions. He also sees our private failures. The greatest thing we can do as believers is walk with God in humility and honesty. When we fail, we should immediately go to him and confess our shortcomings. Today, remember that God sees everything we do, so go to him and he will give you discernment to make wise choices.

RESPONDER'S REFLECTION: The fool says in his heart that there is no God. But greater is the fool who knows there is a God, yet lives like there isn't one.

APRIL 28TH

Psalm 41:10—"Raise me up."

This verse is a great prayer we can pray to God. As some of you are reading today's devotional, you are realizing you need to raise up your expectations. God can raise up your dead dreams. God can raise you up from your worst failures. God can raise you out of debt. God can raise you up from plateauing in life to flourishing. God can raise you out of depression. Let God raise you up!

RESPONDER'S REFLECTION: If you want God to step into some area of your life and help you, just remember: We have to be part of our own rescue. God will raise you up, but he can't help you until you yield to him.

APRIL 29TH

Psalm 46:10 —"Be still, and know that I am God."

Today, some people in the world will wake up glad and others will wake up sad. Regardless of how you may wake up feeling today, I want to draw your attention to an important word in this verse, *still*.

1. God *still* cares for all people.
2. God *still* forgives sin.
3. God *still* restores broken lives.
4. God *still* rescues marriages.
5. God *still* heals our emotions and physical bodies.
6. God *still* loves this world with an unconditional love that led him to give his son Jesus for us.
7. God *still* has a plan for your life and mine.

RESPONDER'S REFLECTION: Regardless of how you may feel today, remember that God is *still* in control.

APRIL 30TH

Proverbs 4:25 —"Let your eyes look straight ahead; fix your gaze directly before you."

Keep your eyes fixed forward on God and his Word. Years ago, a famous footballer running back was about to score a touchdown. However, as he was sprinting toward the end zone, he made a tremendous error…He looked back! A defensive player was chasing him and if he had just continued to look forward, he would have scored a touchdown. Unfortunately, when he looked back, that action slowed him down just enough to be tackled before he could score. Just like this example, God wants you to keep your eyes fixed on him and toward your bright future. God wants you looking forward to his great plans for your life. Look ahead!

RESPONDER'S REFLECTION: You can't live life to the full when you are looking back instead of forward!

MAY 1ST

1 Corinthians 13:8 —"Love never fails."

Have you ever been in your home when a citywide power outage took place? Everything in your home powered by electricity becomes useless. It doesn't matter how expensive the appliance or how trendy the tool, without power it is ineffective! Friend, our lives are the same way without God's love. Everything we have is useless without God! Our talent, our skills, and our wisdom is useless without the love of Jesus. Today, make sure that all you do flows out of God's unconditional love.

RESPONDER'S REFLECTION: We need to make sure to daily plug into our source of life!

MAY 2ND

2 Chronicles 6:4 —"Praise be to the Lord, the God of Israel, who with his hands has fulfilled what he promised with his mouth."

I love how real the Bible is. Don't you wish all people would follow through on what they said they would do? Wouldn't it be nice if our leaders were as faithful to their word as God is to his? As today's verse mentions, God always accomplishes what he says he will do. How many times have we heard promises from others that we knew wouldn't be fulfilled? The good news is every single promise God has made he will fulfill!

RESPONDER'S REFLECTION: God's delay does not mean God's denial. Sometimes, God makes us wait for the promise. Hang in there; God will be faithful to what he promised!

MAY 3RD

Isaiah 43:19 —"Now it springs up; do you not perceive it? I am making a way in the wilderness and streams in the wasteland."

Friend, what problems are you struggling with today? The key to victory in your life is to stop resisting and start receiving. Begin receiving the following from God: His wisdom, the gift of his righteousness, the cleansing power of his forgiveness, and his favor. In order to receive, you must perceive! Do you perceive or comprehend how incredible God's plans are for you? He wants to do amazing things in your life…Can you not perceive it?

RESPONDER'S REFLECTION: In order to receive, you must perceive. Are you positioning yourself to receive from God?

MAY 4TH

John 11:23 —"Jesus said to her, 'Your brother will rise again.'"

Jesus made a promise that no person on Earth could make or keep! He promised to bring a dead man back to life again...and he actually did! Jesus is still in the business of bringing what is dead back to life. Maybe you have a dead marriage, dream, or career, Jesus can bring any of those back to life. No matter what seems lifeless, Jesus can make it alive again. Everything Jesus did in the New Testament, he still does today!

RESPONDER'S REFLECTION: Jesus did not come to Earth to make us better people, but to bring what was dead back to life.

MAY 5TH

John 8:32 —"Then you will know the truth, and the truth will set you free."

If you want freedom and power, then you have to know the truth. One of the greatest mistakes Christians can make is repeating the lies the devil has spoken to them. The more they recite the enemy's words to themselves or others, the more powerless they become. Christians who are changing the world do the opposite. Instead of accepting the lies, they are constantly repeating what God says about them and because they agree with the truth, they are free!

RESPONDER'S REFLECTION: Stop repeating what the devil says about you and start repeating what God says about you.

MAY 6TH

Acts 8:35 — "Then Philip began with that very passage of Scripture and told him the good news about Jesus."

Don't we all love to hear good news? Unfortunately, when we watch TV or read the news, we can get depressed rather quickly! However, God gives us many reasons to have joy! The following are just a few of the many promises Jesus gives us. Jesus promises to:

1. Forgive our sins.
2. Heal us emotionally and physically.
3. Provide for our every need so we don't have to worry.
4. Never leave or forsake us.
5. Strengthen us.
6. Give us his grace and mercy.

Friend, the good news about Jesus is endless! So today, don't get bogged down in the bad news, but instead focus on the good news!

RESPONDER'S REFLECTION: You can't have a positive life if you have a negative mind set. Today focus on God's good news.

MAY 7TH

Joshua 24:15 — "Then choose for yourselves this day whom you will serve."

Life is all about choices. Most people who have blessed lives are the ones who repeatedly make healthy choices. The key to making beneficial choices is to test each choice by asking yourself this one question, "Can I enjoy the choice I make today tomorrow?" Typically, when we make choices we can only enjoy today, we must pay a steep price tomorrow. Choose wisely this day whom and what you will serve.

RESPONDER'S REFLECTION: When you choose to serve God, there is freedom. When you choose to serve yourself, there will always be bondage. The choice is completely up to you.

MAY 8TH

2 Corinthians 12:9 —"My grace is sufficient for you, for my power is made perfect in weakness."

Do you feel weak today? Maybe, you feel drained because you are struggling in some area of your life today. God wants you to know his grace is sufficient for any difficulty you might be facing. In our human wisdom, we think we feel best in our own strength, but the truth is that God can use our lives more through our weaknesses. When we are weak, God is strong! However, sadly the opposite is true as well. When we are strong in ourselves, we will not have true power to live life.

RESPONDER'S REFLECTION: It is in our weakness that people and the world get the best view of God's grace and strength in us. Invite God into your weakness.

MAY 9TH

Psalm 102:1 —"Hear my prayer, Lord."

Have you ever asked someone a question where you already knew what the answer was going to be? On March 13, 2001, I proposed to my then girlfriend, and now wife. I knew when I popped the question, she would answer yes, but I was still very nervous to ask her. Friends, sometimes we act this same way with God. We become nervous when we ask God for what we know he will say yes to. When you pray in line with God and his Word, you can bet your last dollar that God is listening to you and he will answer you with power and love!

RESPONDER'S REFLECTION: God is listening to your prayers. Many times, prayer not only changes our situations, but it also changes us.

MAY 10TH

Galatians 2:21 —"I do not set aside the grace of God."

The greatest gift in life is God's grace! God freely gives it, but many of us don't always freely receive it. Friend, are you judging yourself or someone else too harshly? One of the best things we can do is live in God's grace. If you or someone around you has made mistakes, God wants you to give and receive grace. Don't take life too seriously! Too many times, we judge others by their actions and we judge ourselves by our intentions. We need to strive to live in God's grace and give his grace to others daily.

RESPONDER'S REFLECTION: Too many times, we judge others by their actions and we judge ourselves by our intentions.

MAY 11TH

Daniel 2:28 —"But there is a God in heaven who reveals mysteries."

Are you confused about a situation in your life today? Do you need wisdom on how to make a relationship work? Do you need insight on how to obtain a job or how to overcome a specific problem in your life where you are struggling? Friend, no mystery is too puzzling for God. He can remove your confusion because he wants you to see clearly! If you are in the process of making an important decision, consider this piece of wisdom I once heard my wife say, "If you doubt, don't!" If you aren't sure what to do, wait on and listen for God. He will reveal to you what you need to do.

RESPONDER'S REFLECTION: God's blessing is like an umbrella. As long as you are under the covering, you are safe. However, when you make choices without consulting and hearing from God, you are stepping outside of the protection of the umbrella.

MAY 12TH

Galatians 4:5 —"That we might receive adoption to sonship."

Do you know what your rights are as God's child? Friend, today you have the right to:

1. Enjoy life.
2. Overcome any of the enemy's attacks.
3. Not feel guilty.
4. Live in victory.
5. Be blessed.

Why? Because, when you place your faith in Jesus, you are adopted into his family. Therefore, you get to receive the full rights of being a son or daughter of God.

RESPONDER'S REFLECTION: You have the right to live an abundant life because you are a child of God.

MAY 13TH

Psalm 7:17 —"I will give thanks to the Lord because of his righteousness."

Giving thanks shouldn't just be something we do only during the Thanksgiving holiday. Every day we are alive, regardless of what is going on in our lives, we should be grateful to God! We need to daily thank God for his love, his Son, and the freedoms we have. We should also thank God because he is our loving Father who cares for our every need. Living a life of thankfulness is the breeding ground for blessing.

RESPONDER'S REFLECTION: Thankful lives are blessed ones, while ungrateful lives are lacking.

MAY 14TH

Psalm 121:3 —"He will not let your foot slip."

Are you going through some uncertainty in your life right now? If so, the good news is that God "will not let your foot slip." You could be experiencing some crazy and indecisive times in life, but if your eyes are on the Lord, he will get you through without falling. God's Word is the sturdy foundation on which we can build our lives, dreams, and hopes. As long as you are standing on his Word, you won't lose your footing.

RESPONDER'S REFLECTION: The greatest way to have the power to stand is to kneel at the cross daily. When we think we can handle life all on our own that is when our footing will slip.

MAY 15TH

Philippians 3:21 —"By the power that enables him to bring everything under his control."

Have you ever felt like you have lost all control of your life? Perhaps, your children, emotions, or finances seem completely out of control. Friend, this one verse can change your life in that God wants to bring whatever is troubling you under his control. However, the key is that we can't both have control. Either we let God be in charge or we rule over our own lives. My life is always better when God is in full control and not me!

RESPONDER'S REFLECTION: Either we will let God have control or we will control our own lives, but both of us can't be in charge at the same time.

MAY 16TH

Psalm 18:28 — "My God turns my darkness into light."

Do you feel overwhelmed by pain or conflicts that seem to surround you in darkness? God is so good in that he gives us a promise to turn our darkness into light. Today, do not concede to the negative thoughts that your situation can't or won't change. God is your loving Father who always keeps his Word! When you invite Jesus into your troubles, his light will drive out the darkness!

RESPONDER'S REFLECTION: God's light can turn around any dark situation. If we want the light of God's power in our personal lives, we need to be the ones who turn that light switch on.

MAY 17TH

Psalm 19:7 — "The law of the Lord is perfect, refreshing the soul."

Has someone or something made you weary? Does your soul need to be refreshed? God's lifeline to us is his promise to revive our lives from the things that would burden or wear us down. No matter how exhausting life might be for you today, God wants to renew your strength. In order for God to revitalize you, it is essential to spend time daily connecting with God!

RESPONDER'S REFLECTION: The more time you spend with God, the more refreshed you will be. We don't *have* to spend time with God; we *get* to spend time with God.

MAY 18TH

Colossians 4:18 —"Grace be with you."

Many people today misunderstand the nature or character of God. God is extremely loving and extends grace to every person he has created. If you feel like you have to be perfect to earn God's love, you won't be and will fall short every time. Instead, God desires that we receive his grace each day. God's love is unconditional and his grace is with us when we succeed or when we fail. God is there to cheer you up or pick you up, so be sure to embrace his grace!

RESPONDER'S REFLECTION: We don't receive grace because of our performance in life. We receive grace because of the perfect performance of Jesus dying on the cross for our sins. Grace is a gift bought by the blood of Jesus.

MAY 19TH

1 Thessalonians 1:10 —"Jesus, who rescues us from the coming wrath."

I know it is the month of May, but do you understand the true meaning of Christmas? In its most simple form, Christmas was God's ultimate rescue plan concerning humanity. God sent his son, Jesus, into the world to be born to rescue us from sin, death, hell, and the grave. Are you in need of rescue today? Maybe you are a believer, but you need God's help with a relationship, a job, a financial situation, or some other problem that is overwhelming you. There is good news for you! Because Jesus died and rose from the grave, he has the power to rescue you from any difficulty you might be facing today!

RESPONDER'S REFLECTION: Sometimes we need rescuing from life and our own choices. God sent Jesus in to this world to rescue you, so let him help you today!

MAY 20TH

Psalm 130:8 —"He himself will redeem."

What do you need redeemed today? Have you lost an opportunity, hurt a friendship, or zigged when you should have zagged? God gives us a promise that he is our redeemer. To redeem means to restore or recover. God is in the business of restoring any area of your life that has been damaged, lost or stolen. If God says he will redeem, you can count on him to deliver on his promise! God is faithful to do what he said he would do.

RESPONDER'S REFLECTION: Only God has the power to restore and bring healing to our lives. God can bring back to your life what the enemy has stolen. Let him be your redeemer!

MAY 21ST

1 Thessalonians 3:13 —"May he strengthen your hearts."

God desires to strengthen you. He wants you to be strong in him, in your relationships, and in his vision and plan for your life. One of the ways to become strong is to shut out the negative influences in life. If there are people who have tried to tell you why you can't accomplish or achieve something, let those voices get drowned out by God's voice of encouragement telling you that you can! Let God strengthen your heart today!

RESPONDER'S REFLECTION: It doesn't take a lot of man if God has all the man. The more you surrender to God, the more powerful you will become!

MAY 22ND

1 John 3:1 — "See what great love the Father has lavished on us."

What you yield to, you will be full of. There is no way to get around this truth. If you yield to anger that is what you will be full of. If you yield to anxiety that is what you will be full of. If you yield to prejudice that is what you will be full of. However that can also work for good. If you yield to God's love you will be full of his love. If you yield to God's presence you will be full of his presence. Today make sure you are yielding to the right things.

RESPONDER'S REFLECTION: Are there people you need to stay away from? Are there influences you need to avoid? Make sure you are around sources of God's love.

MAY 23RD

Lamentations 3:22-23 — "For his compassions never fail. They are new every morning."

Have you ever woken up and realized you had a big mess on your hands you had to deal with that day? Or, maybe you have awakened to handling problems caused by your own poor choices. Friend, God promises to give us grace and mercy that is new every day. As you start today, let the fresh love and compassion of God become real to you so that you can overcome any issues you are facing!

RESPONDER'S REFLECTION: God's mercies are new every morning. Each day God gives us a brand new start. No matter what the devil is telling you, you can have a new start today.

MAY 24TH

2 Thessalonians 2:13 — "God chose you."

Low self-esteem issues and arrogance don't blend with God's love. God doesn't want you to see yourself through your own eyes or through the eyes of your family and friends. God wants you to view yourself through his eyes. Friend, God chose you because you are so incredibly valuable to him. God chose to love, bless, prosper, and save you. Today, if you need a pep in your step, ponder this thought that "God chose you"!

RESPONDER'S REFLECTION: Just as God chose you, would you consider choosing someone you can bless who is not able to pay you back?

MAY 25TH

Exodus 14:14 — "The Lord will fight for you; you need only to be still."

God not only wants to be with you throughout your day, but he also wants to fight any battles that would come against you. The key is you need to take time out of your busy life to be still, and let God work on our behalf. Many times, being still is easier said than done, but it sure makes life better when God moves on your behalf. Let God fight for you!

RESPONDER'S REFLECTION: When you let God fight for you, it means you let God be your defender and you don't retaliate when someone else hurts you. Let go and let God fight your battles!

MAY 26TH

Philippians 3:13 —"Forgetting what is behind and straining toward what is ahead."

We all have good and bad things happen to us every day. God wants us to keep and build on the good that happens in our lives. On the contrary, God desires for us to forget the bad that has occurred. God doesn't want the negative incidents that occurred in your past to hamper your future. Today, if you have burdens from the past that are weighing you down, lay those at the feet of your loving Savior!

RESPONDER'S REFLECTION: Too many times, we use the mistakes of the past to pay for our future. Leave the past in the past!

MAY 27TH

Luke 1:37 —"For no word from God will ever fail."

Have you ever heard the expression, "Don't get your hopes up?" Friend, this statement is the exact opposite of what God wants you to do. God wants you to get your hopes up because nothing is impossible with him! Get your hopes up for your relationships, finances, and your future. Remove limitations in your life and believe God by taking him at his Word!

RESPONDER'S REFLECTION: Henry Ford once said, "If you believe you can't do it or if you believe you can; either way, you are right!" What are you going to believe today?

MAY 28TH

Jonah 1:3 — "But Jonah ran away from the Lord."

Stop running from God! Is there an area of your life you won't submit to God? If we would be honest, most of us would have to answer yes. However, when there is an area we don't yield to God, in essence, we are running away from him. In my own personal experience, I have discovered that the things I keep from God always cause me the most pain. If you want a blessed life, don't run from God into a whale of problems but instead, run to him with every problem, hurt, and desire!

RESPONDER'S REFLECTION: The things we keep from God end up hurting us the most. Invite God into your pain.

MAY 29TH

Psalm 39:5 — "Everyone is but a breath."

Wow! This verse will bring you into reality quickly. Tomorrow isn't promised, but even if we were guaranteed 80 years in this life, that timespan is but a breath compared to eternity. Are you going to live life only focused on you, or are you going to live focused on the Lord and helping others? Friend, the emptiest people in this world are the ones who are full of themselves. When we devote our lives to serving God and others, we fully maximize our lives!

RESPONDER'S REFLECTION: Everyone is leaving a legacy with their lives; either by design or by default. What type of legacy will you leave?

MAY 30TH

Luke 12:7 — "Indeed, the very hairs of your head are all numbered."

It is important to take all your needs, regardless of how large or small, to God. Many times, we think we can only pray to God about our big problems, and then neglect to share the smaller ones with him. Friend, if God has taken the time to number all the hairs on your head (including the few hairs I have left on my baldhead) then he has plenty of time to deal with even your small concerns. In fact, he wants to help you solve any problem you are facing. Take all of those issues to our loving God today.

RESPONDER'S REFLECTION: If your small problem bothers you, then it bothers God too. God cares about every part of your life.

MAY 31ST

Hebrews 2:18 — "Because he (Jesus) himself suffered when he was tempted, he is able to help those who are being tempted."

Right now, you may be tempted to do something you know you shouldn't do. Friend, there is a good chance that some temptation may have come to your mind after you read that statement. No matter what the temptation, don't do it! This verse states that Jesus is able to help those who are being tempted. He can help you overcome any temptation that you are struggling with today! The greatest weapon we have to overcome temptation is fleeing. Instead of giving into temptation, we can choose to flee from it!

RESPONDER'S REFLECTION: You have a choice to either feed or starve the daily temptations you face today! Just remember whatever you feed will grow.

JUNE 1ST

Psalm 46:11 — "The Lord Almighty is with us; the God of Jacob is our fortress."

Life can't beat you down! Why? Because of who is with you — God! God gives us an amazing promise that he is not only with us, but goes a step further and states that he is our fortress. A fortress defined is as a place of refuge that offers complete support and protection. Friend, when we go to God, then we receive his complete protection. A fortress won't do us any good if we don't run into it. Therefore, run into God's presence today!

RESPONDER'S REFLECTION: The only way a child of God can be defeated is when they quit. Don't let the devil, a friend, or a family member get you to quit!

JUNE 2ND

2 Corinthians 4:8 — "We are hard pressed on every side, but not crushed."

Our struggles in life produce strength! If you are struggling today, God is not allowing this struggle to harm you, but to strengthen you. Oftentimes, the strongest and most powerful people we know are those who have endured hardships and are now stronger because of it. If you are struggling today, don't ask God to remove the struggle from your life; ask God to help you go through the struggle. When you come out on the other side, you will be stronger not just for your own sake, but for the sake of others.

RESPONDER'S REFLECTION: Our struggles produce strength. Don't ask God to remove your struggles; ask him to help you go through them.

JUNE 3RD

Psalm 45:2 — "God has blessed you forever."

Do you want some great news? God's blessings never run out. He doesn't have a limited supply. Notice that the Bible clearly states, "God has blessed you forever." As you go through your day, I want to encourage you to meditate on Psalm 45:2 and boldly declare aloud, "I am blessed!" Even though all the bad things that happen in our world can bring us discouragement, we need to keep our hearts and minds set on God's many blessings!

RESPONDER'S REFLECTION: There is no expiration date on the blessings of God. The Word of God declares, "God has blessed you forever."

JUNE 4TH

Psalm 48:14 — "For this God is our God for ever and ever; he will be our guide even to the end."

Failing to plan is planning to fail. Do you need a game plan for a situation in your life? Did you have some great goals and ideas, but now find that you are tempted to give up? Friend, God wants to give you his wisdom and direction for your life. What is great about God's wisdom is his guidance and presence is with us until the very end. He will never leave us stranded. Don't give up on your goals!

RESPONDER'S REFLECTION: Failing to plan is planning to fail. Make big plans with God for every area of your life!

JUNE 5TH

Psalm 121:8 —"The Lord will watch over your coming and going both now and forevermore."

Are you aware that you are being watched? Not by Big Brother or an agency that wants to harm you, but by a loving God who wants to pour out his favor and protection on you. It is reassuring to discover that God promises to watch over and protects us "both now and forevermore." Today, grasp this concept that God has his eye on you, not because he is watching to see if you make mistakes, but because he loves you and is for you!

RESPONDER'S REFLECTION: We watch over what we love. God is watching over you!

JUNE 6TH

Ephesians 4:29 —"Do not let any unwholesome talk come out of your mouths, but only what is helpful for building others up according to their needs."

How you describe someone when he or she isn't around speaks more about you than it does that person. The Bible states in Proverbs 18:21 that "the tongue has the power of life and death." Therefore, either our words can bring healing or our words can bring harm. All of us have experienced the joy of encouraging words and the pain of hurtful words. Today, closely examine how you are using your words. Are your words building up or tearing down?

RESPONDER'S REFLECTION: How you describe someone when he or she isn't around speaks more about you than it does that person.

JUNE 7TH

Haggai 1:5 —"Give careful thought to your ways."

When a police officer arrests a criminal, more often than not, the arrested person knows they were breaking the law. When it comes to sin, the same can be said of us too. Typically, when we sin against God, we know that what we are doing is wrong. Is there a sinful action in your life today that God wants you to stop? Listen to the warning again, "Give careful thought to your ways." Friend, if you are doing something you shouldn't be doing, ask God to help you end that behavior now. Take your sins to God and let him get you off the path of destruction and onto the path of blessing.

RESPONDER'S REFLECTION: Don't just make choices and ask God to bless what you are doing. Instead, ask God what choices he will bless, and then make those choices.

JUNE 8TH

Matthew 7:1 —"Do not judge, or you too will be judged."

Do you sometimes find it easy to see the faults in others and judge them? I don't know about you, but sadly, there have been times when I have been critical and judgmental toward others in my heart and mind. However, God isn't pleased when we judge others. He doesn't want us focused on other people's business; he wants us focused on our own business. Today, if you are tempted to judge someone, here is a good rule of thumb, don't do it! Give other people the grace you want to receive.

RESPONDER'S REFLECTION: When we judge others, we slip into one of the most dangerous mindsets, that of self-righteousness.

JUNE 9TH

Psalm 56:3 — "When I am afraid, I put my trust in you."

It doesn't matter how tough you might be, there are times when we all become fearful or afraid. It isn't wrong to be scared, but where we deviate is when we turn to the wrong source during those fearful times. This verse talks about turning to and trusting God when we are afraid. However, sometimes we are tempted to turn to other things such as our own knowledge and experience, substances, money, or something man-made. Friend, we don't have to be afraid of anything as long as our trust is in God.

RESPONDER'S REFLECTION: You can feed your faith or feed your fears. Keep in mind that whatever you feed will grow.

JUNE 10TH

Zechariah 4:6 — "'Not by might nor by power, but by my Spirit,' says the Lord Almighty."

Do you need strength to do the right thing, to live morally, or to believe God for his very best for your life? Friend, we all do! Contrary to our culture's opinion, true life-giving power is not found within ourselves, but instead, only found in God. Today, one of the most powerful statements you can make is, "I can't do it without God's help," because that declaration aligns our minds with the truth that true power only comes from God!

RESPONDER'S REFLECTION: The power you need to live life and overcome the obstacles you could face only comes from God.

JUNE 11TH

Romans 8:28 —"And we know that in all things God works for the good of those who love him."

Have you ever tried to make sense out of life? Sometimes, it can be difficult to try to figure out a relationship, job expectations, how to parent, and so forth. The good news is you don't have to figure everything out! God is the one who makes all things work together for our good and our job is simply to love him. Today, don't try to piece everything together in your life, but instead, strive toward loving God.

RESPONDER'S REFLECTION: The closer you are to God, the more clarity you will have about your life. The further away you are from God, the more confused you will become.

JUNE 12TH

Psalm 60:12 —"With God we will gain the victory, and he will trample down our enemies."

God wants you to have victory! In other words, God wants you to win in life. We all have enemies of worry, fear, and doubt. At times, we yield to thoughts, desires, or actions that we shouldn't. However, God promises us that we will gain the victory when we walk with him. Remember that whatever you are facing in your life today God has already defeated it!

RESPONDER'S REFLECTION: Your problem is a platform for God to demonstrate his power! Whatever you are facing in your life, God has already defeated it.

JUNE 13TH

Psalm 62:1 — "Truly my soul finds rest in God; my salvation comes from him."

Millions of us long to find rest for our souls. There are times when we search in the wrong places to obtain the rest we desperately desire. However, we won't find true rest by going on a vacation, starting a new job, or listening to relaxing music. We can only find genuine rest from the problems we face by running into the loving arms of God. Today, if you are going through a storm in your life, come in out of the rain and into God's rest.

RESPONDER'S REFLECTION: Nothing will wear us out more than to trying to do what only God can do. Let your soul find rest in God alone.

JUNE 14TH

Psalm 65:3 — "When we were overwhelmed by sins, you forgave our transgressions."

Are you feeling overwhelmed today? Have you made a mountain out of a molehill? Sometimes, when we mess up in life, we fall into the trap of thinking our mistakes are beyond fixing. However, that thought is a lie! God gives us a promise that when our sins overwhelm us, his answer is forgiveness. Today, receive the grace and forgiveness of God. Recognize that the blood and sacrifice of Jesus overwhelms all your failures by the power of God.

RESPONDER'S REFLECTION: When you focus on your problems, you will be overwhelmed. When you focus on Jesus, your problems will be overwhelmed.

JUNE 15TH

2 Peter 2:7 — "If he rescued Lot, a righteous man."

God called Lot a righteous man. Why? Not because of Lot's own actions, but because of the grace of God. Our natural tendency is to think that God's blessing is based on our performance. However, we can't earn the blessing of God by our own actions or behavior. Instead, we receive the blessing of God because of his grace. God wants to bless you today, but you can't earn it. The blessing of God is received, not achieved.

RESPONDER'S REFLECTION: Our natural tendency is to believe that our own actions or performance is the basis for God's blessing. However, God's desire to bless us comes from his true heart of love and compassion toward us.

JUNE 16TH

Psalm 66:12 — "You brought us to a place of abundance."

God wants to bring your marriage, relationships, well-being, and personal life to a place of abundance. Abundance means plentiful supply. God is not stingy. In fact, today's verse reminds us about the abundance God wants to give us. Imagine an abundance of peace and strength in your life. The key to having all that God wants you to have is to make sure you are in a place to receive the abundance. That place is putting your faith in God and humbly waiting for him. God hasn't given up on you, so don't give up on him!

RESPONDER'S REFLECTION: God doesn't want you to just get by and live a good-enough life. God wants you to live a more-than-enough life, called the abundant life!

JUNE 17TH

Psalm 68:19 —"Praise be to the Lord, to God our Savior, who daily bears our burdens."

Why are you carrying that burden, care, or problem today? I ask myself this question a lot. However, God does not want us to endure the issues of life on our own. Why? Because he has decided to bear our burdens for us. What I appreciate the most about this promise is that God not only desires to carry the problems we face in life, but he promises to do so on a daily basis! Thank God. Lay those burdens down that God wants to carry for you.

RESPONDER'S REFLECTION: The Lord doesn't want you to carry burdens; he wants you to carry blessings. However, you can't carry both. Which will you choose to carry?

JUNE 18TH

Psalm 69:33 —"The Lord hears the needy."

Have you ever acted like you were listening when someone was talking to you, but in reality you were more focused on something else and didn't hear a word that person said? If we are honest, we can all answer in the affirmative to that question. On the contrary, God is always listening to the pleas, cries, and requests of his children. However, the only way God can't hear us is when we don't call out to him. Today, if you have any need, whether big or small, God is listening and wants to answer you.

RESPONDER'S REFLECTION: The Lord hears you. God sees what is going on in your life. Many times, we want God to answer our prayers instantaneously. However, God's delay does not mean he will deny answering your prayers.

JUNE 19TH

Genesis 2:3 —"He (God) rested from all the work of creating that he had done."

God is often referred to as Creator. Friend, today God can create a job opening, a new friendship, or an opportunity for you to meet a future spouse if you are single. God can also create healing in your body or mind. God is the Creator and is able to create an answer to any problem you are facing. Just because we can't see a possible answer to our problems doesn't mean God can't or won't create an answer. What a mighty and loving God we serve!

RESPONDER'S REFLECTION: Just because we can't see a possible answer to a situation we are facing doesn't mean God can't create an answer out of nowhere!

JUNE 20TH

Psalm 75:7 —"He brings one down, he exalts another."

Do you need an uplift today? God can lift you out of anything. This verse states that God exalts, which means to elevate, raise, or promote. The devil will try to trap us into thinking that we need to turn to other people in order to escape or fix the troubles we encounter. However, only God has all the answers to life's greatest questions and problems. Today let God elevate you above whatever is trying to pull your life down. God wants you to overcome the daily obstacles you face.

RESPONDER'S REFLECTION: No one can keep you from succeeding if you are doing God's will for your life!

JUNE 21ST

Luke 1:37 — "For no word from God will ever fail."

Have you ever met someone you thought you could trust, only to later be disappointed to discover that person to be completely unreliable? At some point in life, we have all depended upon someone we once thought would be there forever only to experience that person abandon us. In contrast, the Word of God will never fail. The promises of the Lord are always trustworthy and consistent. The declarations of Almighty God will not be stopped. You can stand on God's Word and if you do, you won't be defeated.

RESPONDER'S REFLECTION: The Word of God is the final authority, period!

JUNE 22ND

Exodus 14:14 — "The Lord will fight for you; you need only to be still."

We all have to endure the daily battles of life. We may have to battle work, family, health, personal issues or you name whatever else! One of the wonderful things about following the Lord is that he promises to fight for us if we are still. As difficult as it can be, practice being still today and let God fight for you. Be humble with God and others and watch him work on your behalf!

RESPONDER'S REFLECTION: Many times, we try to fix problems on our own, but sometimes, there are things you can't fix or people you can't heal! However, God can fix anything and heal anyone.

JUNE 23RD

Psalm 78:35 — "They remembered that God was their Rock."

Isn't it frustrating when we forget? There may be times when we forget some important items such as our cell phone, wallet, driver's license, money, or car keys. Sadly, there may be times when we have even forgotten about God. As you start a busy new day, don't forget to connect with God, the most important relationship you have in life. God is our rock and with him, we can stand against any test this life tries to throw our way. Today, remember you need God in everything you do, in every decision you make, and in every relationship you encounter. Remember God!

RESPONDER'S REFLECTION: We need God in every area of our lives, so don't forget to connect with him today!

JUNE 24TH

Psalm 121:1 — "I lift up my eyes to the mountains—where does my help come from?"

One of the greatest tricks the devil will try to perform on us is to mess with our vision. He will attempt to get our eyes turned backwards where we focus on our past. If he isn't successful in doing that, he will try to get us to turn our eyes downward in shame over our sins and struggles. However, God has a completely different approach! Instead, God wants you to lift up your eyes. He wants you to look up to him for help. God wants you to lift your eyes to a bright and exciting future. He also desires that you look up and forward to victory in your life! Isn't God good?

RESPONDER'S REFLECTION: You can't have an abundant life if you are looking at any place other than looking up to the Lord.

JUNE 25TH

Philippians 3:14 — "I press on toward the goal to win the prize for which God has called me heavenward in Christ Jesus."

Is there an obstacle in the way of one of your dreams? Press on! Does your marriage have a little turbulence right now? Press on! Are you working tirelessly at your job but one problem after another gets in the way of you accomplishing your goals? Press on! Are you finding it challenging to follow God's plans for your life? Press on! God has a reward for each of us if we will just continue to press on!

RESPONDER'S REFLECTION: Anybody can quit. It takes spiritual tenacity and character to press on.

JUNE 26TH

Matthew 11:28 — "Come to me, all you who are weary and burdened, and I will give you rest."

Are you weary today and need rest? Do you need rest from a stressful job, an overwhelming situation, or maybe rest from a person? This verse teaches that God will give you rest especially if you are weary and burdened, but God specifically states to "come to me." Notice that God gives you an invitation for rest, but it is for those who will come and meet God. If you need rest, be assured you won't find it in money, position, power, or things. Today, come to God with your requests and get some rest!

RESPONDER'S REFLECTION: We can only find rest for our souls in the one who created our souls. If you are looking for rest in anything but God, you are wasting your time.

JUNE 27TH

Psalm 83:18 — "That you alone are the Most High over all the earth."

Would you sometimes describe yourself as self-centered? I think if we are honest with ourselves, we can all admit that we tend to be selfish and self-absorbed at times! However, if we want to be blessed in life, we need to focus on God and others above ourselves. Today, whether you are having a difficult or good day, remember that God is Most High over all the earth. He is over everything and is Sovereign! We can rest, be free from worry, and overcome anything because we are his children and he is over all things!

RESPONDER'S REFLECTION: The key to fulfillment and changing the world is to make the transition from having a self-centered life to a God-centered life.

JUNE 28TH

Proverbs 18:10 — "The name of the Lord is a fortified tower; the righteous run to it and are safe."

When we are with God, we are safe. However, sometimes people crawl along or slowly walk to God instead of running to him with their problems. Friend, don't waste any more time! If you are in need of wisdom, healing, or God's help in a certain area, run to God! Every moment you attempt to fix your own problems is a waste of time. Run to God because he will help you and provide for your every need!

RESPONDER'S REFLECTION: Do you run to God or other people for help? Do you turn to God as your source or the fading things of this Earth? Today, choose to run into the safe arms of God!

JUNE 29TH

Matthew 13:15 —"For this people's heart has become calloused."

Sadly, just as this verse indicates, I have allowed my heart to become calloused. There have been times where I have allowed the hurts inflicted by others or my own mistakes to harden my heart. You know your heart is becoming calloused if you:

1. Have trouble forgiving others
2. Hold grudges
3. Live in the past
4. Become apathetic toward the suffering of others
5. Can't forgive yourself

Friend, God's grace is for you and if your heart is calloused, let the grace of God do heart surgery on you today.

RESPONDER'S REFLECTION: Our hearts can only be healed and healthy when completely surrendered to God.

JUNE 30TH

Deuteronomy 5:33 —"Walk in obedience to all that the Lord your God has commanded you, so that you may live and prosper and prolong your days in the land that you will possess."

One time, I received a call from NBC and they invited me to be on the TV show called *Deal or No Deal*. They asked me to be one of the supporters for a friend of mine who played the game. The whole principle of this show was that when you got a good deal, take it! In this verse, God promises an amazing deal. First, he promises life, then prosperity and lastly, long life. Doesn't that sound like a good deal? However, many people choose to turn it down. In order to get that deal, you must "walk in obedience to all that the Lord your God has commanded you." Today, take the deal God is offering to you!

RESPONDER'S REFLECTION: The Lord is offering us abundant life, but sadly, many people turn his deal down. Choose life!

JULY 1ST

Matthew 3:17 —"This is my Son, whom I love; with him I am well pleased."

Today's verse is what God said immediately after John the Baptist baptized Jesus. Notice he states, "This my Son, whom I love; with him I am well pleased." At this point, Jesus had not yet performed any miracles such as healing the lame, raising the dead, or feeding the thousands. What is the point? God loved Jesus and was well pleased with him before he *did* anything! The same is true for us. God does not base his love for us on our performance, but instead, on our position as his sons and daughters. You can't earn God's love because he gives it freely!

RESPONDER'S REFLECTION: God does not base his love for us on our performance, but instead, he loves us because we are his sons and daughters.

JULY 2ND

John 14:1 —"Do not let your hearts be troubled. You believe in God; believe also in me."

My wife and I enjoy getting away and going on vacation. Trips are a great way for us to get some rest and relaxation! However, even though vacations can provide rest and refreshment, they don't necessarily bring our hearts lasting peace. True peace that resides in our hearts and souls can only be found when we meet with God. He is the only one who can genuinely say, "Do not let your hearts be troubled." This statement is true because he is the only one with that type of power. Today, spend time in God's presence and let his peace reside in you!

RESPONDER'S REFLECTION: Peace with God is a personal choice. We can let our hearts be full of joy or full of anxiety. Which will you choose today?

JULY 3RD

Matthew 6:33 —"But seek first his kingdom and his righteousness."

Will you seek God today? Regardless of whether you decide to seek him or not, he is seeking you! In fact, the truth is we will never pursue God as strongly and passionately as he pursues us. Why? Because God created us to be in relationship with him. He desires to walk with us, love us, and know us intimately. Today, don't run from God, run to him. He wants to lead your life on an incredible journey.

RESPONDER'S REFLECTION: Consider this thought that we will never pursue God as strongly and passionately as he pursues us.

JULY 4TH

Genesis 21:1 — "The Lord did for Sarah what he had promised."

Today's verse is so contrary to what we experience in this day and age. How many times have you met people who made empty promises they never intended to keep? Maybe, you were that person who didn't follow through on a promise you made. On the contrary, God always delivers on his promises. If he said it, he will do it! Friend, the good news is God is consistent and never changing. He has promised to heal, forgive, sustain, and bless us. Today, if it seems like God isn't answering a prayer of yours, remember that God is not on our timetable. God is seldom early, but he is never late.

RESPONDER'S REFLECTION: Even though this advice is sometimes easier said than done, don't get inpatient with God! Remember that the Lord is seldom early, but he is never late.

JULY 5TH

Psalm 100:5 — "For the Lord is good and his love endures forever."

Life is worth living because God is good! Notice this verse does not say God does good things, even though he does every day, but it says, "The Lord is good." The very nature of God is goodness. Friend, if we will daily give God our lives, dreams, fears, and pains, he has the power to turn any bad or harmful experience around for good. Reflect on this one thought that God is good and he always has your best interest at heart!

RESPONDER'S REFLECTION: The problem many of us have is when we give God our hurt and pain, oftentimes, we try to take it back. Be sure to leave your troubles with God and let him turn your situation around for good!

JULY 6TH

Psalm 103:2 —"Praise the Lord, my soul, and forget not all his benefits."

We all have a tendency to forget important information from time to time. As life gets busy, it is easy to forget all the benefits God gives his children. The following are ones worth remembering:

1. Total forgiveness of all our sins
2. Freedom from guilt
3. New hope and a future
4. Healing in the deepest areas of our life
5. Peace in the midst of life's storms
6. Unconditional love and acceptance
7. Power to overcome any roadblock

This list could go on and on, so as you get ready for your day, don't forget the benefits of being in the family of God.

RESPONDER'S REFLECTION: Just as eating nutritious foods gives you the natural benefits of being healthy and losing weight, drawing near to God will always give you supernatural benefits.

JULY 7TH

Proverbs 16:3 — "Commit to the Lord whatever you do, and he will establish your plans."

Do you want the ultimate insurance policy? What about the best warranty? Every year, people spend millions on insurance and warranties to ensure they are covered. However, if you want to make sure you succeed in this life, you must commit to the Lord your marriage, job, money, relationships, or you name it. Today, if there is an area of your life that is struggling, perhaps you need to recommit it to God. The good news is God wants you blessed in every area of your life.

RESPONDER'S REFLECTION: There is a world of difference between conveniently coming to the Lord and committing ourselves to the Lord.

JULY 8TH

Romans 8:31 — "If God is for us, who can be against us?"

Nothing can stop you! Yes, you read this statement correctly. Nothing can hinder you if God is for you. Friend, sometimes we make choices based on whether or not we have enough power and strength on our own. However, it is not wise to base our decisions on what we think we can or can't do. We should start making choices, dreams, and visions based on the power that God wants to give each one of us. Today, don't buy into the devil's lie that your desires can't come to pass. God is for you!

RESPONDER'S REFLECTION: Let this thought sink in that God is for you. The biggest question you need to ask yourself is, are you for God?

JULY 9TH

Psalm 107:1 —"His love endures forever."

Everything in this world will eventually break down or will need replacing. Why? Because things are created by human beings. But the love of God endures forever. Why? Because God is the author and creator of love. Today, rest in the fact of knowing that God's intense love for you is never-ending. The love of God endures through any of the difficult times you may face in life!

RESPONDER'S REFLECTION: This world will eventually pass away, but God's love for us is limitless!

JULY 10TH

Genesis 26:12 —"Isaac planted crops in that land and the same year reaped a hundredfold, because the Lord blessed him."

Are you broke and empty? This question is not just about your financial situation, but are you broke in relationships? Are you broke spiritually and don't have any peace to sleep? In today's verse, Isaac received one hundred times blessing from God. What steps did he take? First, he sowed seed where he had need and secondly, he waited for God to bless him. Today, if you have a need in a relationship, bless that other person even if they don't deserve it. If you have trials at work, be the best employee you can be even through the trying times. If you sow seed and commit it to God, you can receive a huge increase as well!

RESPONDER'S REFLECTION: Are you asking big? Are you believing big? Are you envisioning big? God wants you to get your hopes up!

JULY 11TH

Psalm 106:24 — "They did not believe his promise."

If you purchase an airline ticket to fly, you will never arrive at your destination until you have faith to go from the ticket counter to the gate to redeem your ticket and board the plane. After you have completed those steps, only then will you arrive at your final destination. In the same way, God has given you numerous promises of his favor, blessing, and power but you have to believe those promises with your actions. When you have faith and act upon God's Word, you are actually putting legs to your prayers.

RESPONDER'S REFLECTION: The reason your prayers might be unanswered is that God may want you to put legs on those prayers and take action!

JULY 12TH

Psalm 118:24 — "The Lord has done it this very day; let us rejoice today and be glad."

Today is a great day, but perhaps you don't feel like it is because you are currently going through a difficult trial in your life. Friend, regardless of what you might be encountering, today is awesome because God made this very day! If he made today, then he can create answers to any problem you are facing. Don't forget that God never forgets you! Enjoy today and the fact that you are alive even to have problems.

RESPONDER'S REFLECTION: Rejoice and be glad that God has given you this day to be alive and make a difference in this world!

JULY 13TH

Psalm 108:4 —"Your faithfulness reaches to the skies."

Has anyone ever disappointed and let you down? Have you ever counted on another person, company, or church and then suddenly realized they were not following through on what they said they would do? We can all respond to those questions with a resounding, *yes*! In contrast, God is always faithful to love and help us, so much so that his "faithfulness reaches to the skies." That description demonstrates just how trustworthy and faithful God is toward us! Trust God today with every need you have!

RESPONDER'S REFLECTION: Oftentimes, when a friend promises to do something for us, we thank them in advance. If we can trust our friends, how much more should we trust God? Would you consider thanking God in advance for answering your prayers? Remember that God is faithful!

JULY 14TH

Mark 10:9 —"Therefore what God has joined together, let no one separate."

Normally, the words fight and marriage don't go together well. While most people don't need encouragement to fight in their marriages, many people at some point need encouragement to fight for their marriages. If we truly believe that marriage is important, then we need to be warriors for our marriages. Too often, we are passive bystanders allowing the enemies of busyness, selfishness, and pride win battles God has equipped us to win. God wants our relationships blessed, but we need to put our relationship with him first.

RESPONDER'S REFLECTION: While most people don't need encouragement to fight in their marriages, virtually all people at some point need encouragement to fight for their marriages. You marriage is worth fighting for!

JULY 15TH

Luke 15:20 — "But while he was still a long way off, his father saw him and was filled with compassion for him; he ran to his son, threw his arms around him and kissed him."

In this Bible story, what happened when the prodigal son sinned and made major mistakes? The Bible mentions that his father ran to him! Yes, this is true! But his father didn't run to him to punish or harm his son. He ran to him filled with love and compassion. In the same way, when we make mistakes and turn to God for forgiveness, our Heavenly Father runs to us to restore and heal our lives. If you are running away from the love of God, stop running and let God catch up to you and put his arms around you!

RESPONDER'S REFLECTION: When you fail, God is running to restore you, not to punish you.

JULY 16TH

Genesis 26:22 — "We will flourish in the land."

God's will for your life and mine is for us to "flourish in the land." Too many times, we just get by in our marriages, our jobs, and with our dreams. However, God desires more for us than just scraping by because he wants us to flourish. The key word in today's verse is *we* because it means God and us. We can't try to live life without him. We must live life with him. If we will partner with God, we will flourish.

RESPONDER'S REFLECTION: No one is responsible for your response except you. Only you can control how you will respond to God.

JULY 17TH

Psalm 111:9 — "He provided redemption for his people."

Too many times, we tell God how big our problems are, but we need to start telling our problems how big our God is! God is our provider. Whatever you might be going through today, God has already provided. This verse gives us a promise that God will provide for our needs and he will redeem his people. If you need a fresh start in your career, family, friendships, or finances, the good news is that God can redeem and turn around any mistakes you have made! Regardless of trials or issues you may see in your life don't forget God has already provided!

RESPONDER'S REFLECTION: Too many times, we tell God how big our problems are, but we need to start telling our problems how big our God is! He has already provided for our needs!

JULY 18TH

Zephaniah 3:20 — "'When I restore your fortunes before your very eyes,' says the Lord."

God makes an incredible claim here in that he will restore what has been lost or stolen in our lives. Recently, a professional football player was ruled down at the one-yard line, but then after further review of the play, the officials reversed their call and ruled it a touchdown instead. God does the same for us. When we have missed opportunities to be a good spouse, to encourage others, or to help someone, God can restore those situations. If you feel like the devil has stolen something like a relationship or a dream, there are no limits on what God can restore. The only key is that we must let God bring restoration.

RESPONDER'S REFLECTION: God can't restore what you have not given to him.

JULY 19TH

Ephesians 4:15 — "Instead, speaking the truth in love."

A private faith is a powerless faith! As believers in Jesus, we have the greatest message the world has ever seen or heard. Can you imagine creating a cure for cancer and not telling anyone? That is what we do as believers when we don't tell others about Jesus. If Jesus has saved you and forgiven you, you have a supernatural message. We have what this world needs! When you are bold for Jesus and share his message, please make sure that you share it in love. If you have the right message and the wrong spirit, people won't listen to you and lives will never be changed.

RESPONDER'S REFLECTION: A private faith is a powerless faith! Be bold with the gospel of Jesus and share that gospel in love.

JULY 20TH

Colossians 3:2 — "Set your minds on things above, not on earthly things."

Sometimes, I hate to watch the news because the stories that are covered seem to emphasize the negative without much focus on the positive. I am not suggesting that we simply ignore the problems of life, but sometimes focusing on the negative can drag us down. Today, set your minds on things above, which means to focus on God's grace, mercy, love, and his desire to bless you. Promise yourself that in today's negative world, you will be a positive force by focusing on the good things in life and not all the bad!

RESPONDER'S REFLECTION: Setting your mind on negative, earthly things is the easier and more popular thing to do in our culture. However, if you want to be a leader who is different from the rest of this world, set your mind on the positive and good things above.

JULY 21ST

Psalm 119:31 — "I hold fast to your statutes, Lord."

Hold on! This phrase is what I told myself when my wife and I were on a vacation, riding on a banana boat being pulled at high speeds through the ocean. I knew if I could just hold on, I would be fine. Friend, today's word for you is to hold on. If God has given you a dream, hold on to it. If God has given you a promise of his goodness, hold on to that word. If you know God has something better for your life, hold on to that desire. If you will hold fast, or in other words, hold on to what God has promised for your life, you will be blessed.

RESPONDER'S REFLECTION: It takes real courage to hold on to God's promises when you don't see them materializing yet.

JULY 22ND

Romans 5:20 — "But where sin increased, grace increased all the more."

Do you have an accurate view of God? Sometimes, we view God through the lens of him being an overly critical father who wants to condemn us for any wrong move we make. If you only view God as a strict judge who wants to punish you every time you make a mistake, you have an incorrect view. This verse teaches, "Where sin increased, grace increased all the more." Therefore, cut yourself some slack! You can't and won't ever be perfect on this Earth! Do most of us want to make good and moral choices? Yes, of course! However, when you fall short and sin, don't forget that God's love and grace abounds more than any of the mistakes you have made!

RESPONDER'S REFLECTION: A popular acronym for the word Grace is God's Riches At Christ's Expense.

JULY 23RD

Lamentations 3:22-23 —"For his compassions never fail. They are new every morning."

Good morning! Sometimes, I have to make that declaration in faith because by nature, I am not a morning person. In fact, when I was newly married to my wife, I told her not to expect me to talk much when I first woke up. However, the truth is that every morning is a good morning. Why? Because God promises that his compassion and mercy for our life and everything we go through is brand new each morning! No matter what happened yesterday, thank God we have a fresh start today.

RESPONDER'S REFLECTION: Great is God's faithfulness even when we aren't faithful.

JULY 24TH

John 3:16 —"For God so loved the world that he gave his one and only Son, that whoever believes in him shall not perish but have eternal life."

God is the ultimate giver! He gave the greatest gift we could ever receive, which was his son, Jesus. Not only that, he continues to give his grace, mercy, peace, strength, and love to us every day. God wants us to follow his example because we are never more like God than when we give. It is God's nature to be a giver because that is who he is. Today, follow God's heart and give the love of God to those around you.

RESPONDER'S REFLECTION: You are never more like God than when you give. If you want to be a chip off the old block, help people who can't pay you back.

JULY 25TH

Psalm 119:45 — "I will walk about in freedom."

Are you walking in freedom today? Are you living free from worry, anxiety, fear, or gloom? God wants you to be free! God has given power to those who put their faith in him. Not superficial churchy power, but supernatural life-changing power. If you are in bondage in a certain area of your life, God wants you to know he has set you free! Now, you just need to decide to walk in his freedom. Be determined to be blessed and free with God's help!

RESPONDER'S REFLECTION: Many times, we want freedom and power in our lives, but we are unwilling to make changes or do things differently. If you want different, then do different!

JULY 26TH

Acts 13:43 — "Urged them to continue in the grace of God."

Today, continue to stay in the race! Every day, we face distractions that will try to pull us away from God and his purposes, plans, and blessings for our lives. Don't give in and don't give up on God! At times, we can be tempted to quit seeking after God. But remember, God has amazing plans for your life! Continue to trust God. Continue to speak faith. Continue to believe for the impossible. Continue living in God's grace.

RESPONDER'S REFLECTION: When we face adversity, the greatest thing we can do is just continue.

JULY 27TH

Isaiah 43:19 — "See, I am doing a new thing! Now it springs up; do you not perceive it?"

A vision without a plan isn't a dream, but a nightmare! Countless people have dreams but for many they never become a reality. How do you make your dreams become a reality? We need to follow the ABC's of life:

- Attitude…If our attitude stinks, our life will stink.
- Behavior…Until your beliefs become your behaviors, you will never experience life change.
- Choice…You can choose to become a victim or a victor, but you can't be both.

RESPONDERS REFLECTION: A vision without a plan isn't a dream, but a nightmare! Align your attitudes, behaviors, and choices with God's and your dreams will become reality!

JULY 28TH

Psalm 103:10 — "He does not treat us as our sins deserve."

There are numerous reasons why God is so good! A few to consider is that God's love is unconditional, his mercy is unending, his power knows no limits, and his wisdom can't be fully understood by man. However, the one truth we can add to this list is that "He does not treat us as our sins deserve." When we sin, we actually deserve God's wrath and punishment, but this verse expresses that when we fail or fall short, God chooses to show us mercy and forgive us. As you go about this day, remember that God gives us what we don't deserve, which is his love and grace!

RESPONDER'S REFLECTION: Judgment is giving another the punishment they deserve; whereas, grace is giving another unmerited favor or something they don't deserve.

JULY 29TH

Genesis 19:26 — "But Lot's wife looked back, and she became a pillar of salt."

One of the devil's greatest tricks is to try to get us to look back. He wants us to focus on our past hurts, failures, and defeats. But can I give you this one thought? The only time you should ever look back is to see how far you have come. God is more concerned with where you are going than with where you have been. One way the devil will attack us is by attempting to get us to live in the past. Don't look back, but instead, focus on the victory and blessings of God that are in store for you.

RESPONDER'S REFLECTION: Don't live in the past! The only time you should look back is to see how far you have come.

JULY 30TH

Psalm 27:14 — "Wait for the Lord; be strong and take heart."

God is not keeping you from something; he is keeping you for something! Many times, we struggle to wait on God because we grow inpatient. However, if God has you waiting, there is a reason. If you are waiting on a financial breakthrough, don't quit. If you are waiting on that future spouse, don't give up. If you are believing God for some type of physical or emotional healing, hang in there. Whatever you are waiting on God for, just remember that he is not keeping you from something, he is keeping you for something.

RESPONDER'S REFLECTION: The devil wants you to get ahead of God. No matter what lies the devil is telling you, don't stop waiting on God. God is not keeping you from something; he is keeping you for something.

JULY 31ST

Psalm 129:2 —"They have greatly oppressed me from my youth, but they have not gained the victory over me."

Has something been plaguing you for a while? Maybe, you feel like you have battled and been weighed down by the same issue for a very long time with no sign of relief. Today could be your day to get the victory over an attitude, addiction, circumstance, or you name it. Victory is yours to be gained, but just don't quit! Make up your mind today that you will win. Today, determine that you will be blessed and that you will be better than ever.

RESPONDER'S REFLECTION: It's okay if you are living with a problem right now, but just don't let the problem live in you.

AUGUST 1ST

Acts 20:35 —"The Lord Jesus himself said: 'It is more blessed to give than to receive.'"

When is the best time to give to others? Truthfully, the answer is anytime. However, one of the greatest times to give is when we are personally experiencing a difficult time ourselves. This notion may seem counterintuitive, but if you are struggling in some area, don't focus on what you can do for yourself; instead, discover ways where you can bless another person. When we shift our attention off ourselves and onto others with the intention to bless them, God not only blesses them, but us as well!

RESPONDER'S REFLECTION: When we are hurting in life, the devil wants us focused on our own problems. However, one of the quickest ways to be healed from those hurts is to start letting God use our lives to minister to others.

AUGUST 2ND

Joshua 1:5 — "I will never leave you nor forsake you."

Wow, what a wonderful promise from God! Perhaps the most incredible part of this promise is that among the billions of people who live in this world, only God can make and keep such a promise. As much as I love my wife, I can't always be there for her. As much as you love your family, you can't always be there for them. Friend, God wants you to know that he will never leave you nor forsake you. This fact alone should give you courage to live your life in total victory today!

RESPONDER'S REFLECTION: The only person on this planet who can make the promise that he will never leave or forsake us and keep it, is God.

AUGUST 3RD

Romans 5:1 — "Therefore, since we have been justified through faith, we have peace with God through our Lord Jesus Christ."

Peace — the rich can't buy it, the educated can't create it, and the lucky can't find it. God can only give peace for our lives. We obtain this peace when we put our faith in what Jesus did for us when he died on the cross. If you feel guilty for your sins, place your faith in the sacrifice Jesus made on your behalf and begin believing that he has justified and forgiven you. If you are overwhelmed with anxiety, place your faith in God's promises for your life to bring you encouragement. We can't be perfect, but we can have peace by giving our issues to God and placing our faith in the only One who is perfect.

RESPONDER'S REFLECTION: Having peace in our lives is about placing our faith in Jesus because of what he has already accomplished on the cross.

AUGUST 4TH

Psalm 131:2 — "But I have calmed and quieted myself."

How often do you get peace and quiet in your life? It is important to take a break because we all need rest from the daily grind. We need times of being still because if we are not careful, we can become overwhelmed with stress and worry from the trivial hassles we face each day. However, the greatest reason we need to retreat to a peaceful and quiet place is so that we can hear when the Lord speaks to us about his love and direction for our lives. You don't need to go on a vacation or get out of town, but we all need to still our hearts and hear from God.

RESPONDER'S REFLECTION: God is always talking, but the issues of life can be so loud that we can't hear what he is saying. We have to still our souls and turn down the volume of life so that we can hear what God is trying to tell us.

AUGUST 5TH

Psalm 27:1 — "The Lord is my light and my salvation—whom shall I fear?"

Have you ever stubbed your toe in the dark? If you have ever had that experience before, you probably learned to move slower in the dark and stretch your arms out as far as you could to avoid injury again. This example is a picture of how all of us can be sometimes when we are wounded in life and then become fearful. Friend, if you need God to turn the light on in some area of your life, all you need to do is go to him in prayer. Instead of stubbing your toe in the dark, you can run freely into God's light without fear!

RESPONDER'S REFLECTION: Many times, we do something and then ask God to bless what we are doing. However, we need to start asking God what he will bless and then do that instead. We all need the light of God's wisdom.

AUGUST 6TH

Revelation 3:20 —"Here I am! I stand at the door and knock. If anyone opens the door, I will come in and eat with that person, and they with me."

Are you beginning a new phase of life? Perhaps, you may be transitioning from one job to another or you might be stepping out in faith to start a new ministry. Have you ever heard the phrase, "When God closes one door, he opens another?" Friend, also consider this thought that frustration or dismay can occur in the hallway before you open that next door. Today, if you are currently in one of the hallways of life, stand on the promise that when you open the door to the presence and power of God, he will come in!

RESPONDER'S REFLECTION: Your pastor, friends, or even God can't open the door of your heart. You are the only one who can open the door of your heart to God.

AUGUST 7TH

1 Timothy 6:12 —"Fight the good fight of the faith."

Anything worth having in life, you will have to fight for it. If you want to earn that degree, acquire that job, lose those extra pounds, have a blessed marriage, or attain anything else of value, chances are it won't always come easy. Friend, I want to encourage you to only accept God's very best for your life and don't settle for second best in any area! As today's verse states, "Fight the good fight of the faith," so stay in the ring and just know that what you are fighting for will be worth it!

RESPONDER'S REFLECTION: Typically, the things that come easy are of little value. There can't be a testimony without a test. Fight the good fight!

AUGUST 8TH

Hebrews 3:1 — "Fix your thoughts on Jesus."

We all need to take control of our thoughts. Almost any criminal or sinful action starts with an erroneous thought. If we continuously feed that wrong thought, we become more susceptible to act upon it and commit the sin or make the mistake. On the contrary, begin to "fix your thoughts on Jesus." The more you fix your thoughts on Jesus, the more you will see the need to love others unconditionally, to treat others better than yourself, and the less likely you are to pass judgment. When you fix your thoughts on Jesus, you begin to understand what is truly valuable and important in life.

RESPONDER'S REFLECTION: You can't change your life if you don't change your thinking.

AUGUST 9TH

Psalm 121:3 — "He who watches over you will not slumber."

God is always watching! Sometimes, people teach this truth about God's watchful eye to scare and warn people. However, on the other side of the coin, if God is always watching over you, then he sees when you need wisdom, when you are hurt, when you are confused, and he always knows exactly what you need. Friend, God is watching your back! Today, trust him and rest in his protection.

RESPONDER'S REFLECTION: God watches over you because he loves you and wants the best for your life. Trust him to take care of your every need.

AUGUST 10TH

Psalm 135:5 —"Our Lord is greater than all gods."

In our secular society, many people serve different gods other than the One and only God. Some people serve the god of money, or the god of fame, or the god of people's approval. We could easily name more idols because the list is long. The problem is that all those gods are artificial and empty. However, our Heavenly Father is the all-powerful, all-knowing, and loving God. As you go through this day, don't allow yourself to bow down to other gods. Put your hope and faith in the Lord, the only ever-loving eternal God!

RESPONDER'S REFLECTION: It is very easy to determine what god we are serving. Whatever controls you, that is your god. Make sure it is the creator that is guiding you and not the created. The Lord wants to be your God.

AUGUST 11TH

Exodus 4:31 —"And when they heard that the Lord was concerned about them and had seen their misery, they bowed down and worshiped."

God is concerned about you! He sees everything you face and he understands everything you experience. God's heart is moved with compassion and love for you. Our response toward the Lord should be the same as the people in this verse in that we should bow down and worship him today. What you worship determines what you value. It takes boldness to worship God in front of others. Stand up for God today by bowing down and worshipping him because he deserves it!

RESPONDER'S REFLECTION: What you worship determines what you value. What do you value?

AUGUST 12TH

Ephesians 2:14 — "For he himself is our peace."

What has stolen your peace of mind? Has your peace been robbed by an unexpected bill, a stressful situation at your job, or maybe a disagreement with a family member? Friend, I have good news! Jesus himself is our peace and he will never leave us. Focusing on what has stolen your peace won't bring the peace you desire to have. In order to have peace, your focus needs to be solely on Jesus, the Prince of Peace.

RESPONDER'S REFLECTION: You can never have true peace in your life if Jesus Christ is not your first priority. If your relationship with God is on the back burner, you will never have the amazing peace God wants you to have. Remember that Jesus is your peace.

AUGUST 13TH

Exodus 5:3 — "The God of the Hebrews has met with us."

It is the desire of my heart to daily meet with God. I don't want to just talk about God or listen to worship songs about him, but I want to be in his presence and actually spend time with him. Friend, each of us can meet with God in a real and personal way. Every day God gives us a personal invitation to know him and walk with him. We receive power to live life and overcome every obstacle when we meet with him. Today, don't reject God's invitation for you to spend time in his presence.

RESPONDER'S REFLECTION: All religions except Christianity focus on man trying to reach up to connect with God. Christianity is about God reaching down to connect with man. God wants to meet with you today.

AUGUST 14TH

Psalm 141:8 — "But my eyes are fixed on you, Sovereign Lord."

Have you ever heard an athletic coach say, "Keep your eyes forward"? Why would a coach use this expression to motivate players? Because the only way to win is to keep your eyes fixed on the finish line or prize. The same is true in life. There are times when disruptions sneak into your life that would attempt to get your eyes off God. Don't let yourself become distracted! More times than not, the majority of mistakes we make occur when we take our eyes off God. God's eyes are always on us, so let's always keep our eyes on him.

RESPONDER'S REFLECTION: What your eyes are focused on shows others what you value.

AUGUST 15TH

Matthew 7:7 — "Ask and it will be given to you."

How big is your ask? The Bible clearly states that God is willing to answer your prayers, but do you have the faith to ask him abundant-sized prayers? Today, let your ask grow and begin to believe God for things you don't even think are possible! When you make your requests to God, are you asking big enough? When it comes to your prayer life, it is better to err on the side of asking God for too much than not enough. God wants you to believe and ask big!

RESPONDER'S REFLECTION: How big is your ask?

AUGUST 16TH

Psalm 103:2-3 — "Forget not all his benefits—who forgives all your sins."

What a powerful promise! A close friend of mine who is a Kansas City Missouri Police Officer once shared with me the following insight he had about God's forgiveness: "A court of law promises a trial with an unknown outcome. God promises an immediate trial with a known outcome." I couldn't have said it better myself. The bottom line is that the Judge and Creator of this entire world wants you to know that one of the many benefits of being a Christ follower is that he will forgive all your sins. I like God's courtroom!

RESPONDER'S REFLECTION: A court of law promises a trial with an unknown outcome. God promises an immediate trial with a known outcome that he forgives you.

AUGUST 17TH

Romans 11:20 — "You stand by faith."

Faith is not believing God can, faith is believing God will. There is no way for this life to be perfect! Therefore, what should you do when your dreams are under attack or you start to feel like you just can't win? The answer is to stand in faith. Put your faith in God to give you his wisdom, strength, courage, healing, love, or anything else you may need. Make your requests to God and believe he will move on your behalf. If we don't stand in faith, we will sit in doubt and never accomplish the plans God has for our life. Stand in faith today!

RESPONDER'S REFLECTION: Faith is not believing God can, but believing God will. If we don't stand in faith, we will sit in doubt.

AUGUST 18TH

Romans 12:17 — "Do not repay anyone evil for evil."

Romans 12:21— "Do not be overcome by evil, but overcome evil with good."

Is evil attacking you? Are there people or situations trying to bring distress or pain into your life? Perhaps the attack is coming from a family member, or department politics at your job, or someone you know from church. The way you overcome these kinds of attacks is not by fighting fire with fire, but by giving the goodness of God to others. We can overcome any assault against us if we choose not to get revenge, but instead let God's love pour out of us. If you feel attacked today, don't give up and don't fight with your own power. Instead, give out the love of God!

RESPONDER'S REFLECTION: If you fight fire with fire, everyone gets burned.

AUGUST 19TH

Romans 13:14 — "Clothe yourselves with the Lord Jesus Christ."

Have you ever had to wear sweaty, dirty clothes after working hard because you were short on time and couldn't change into a clean outfit? If so, you were probably uncomfortable, you may have reeked, or you might have been embarrassed. Today and every day, God wants us to clothe ourselves with Jesus. He wants us to put on the same attitude, love, and grace as Jesus. When we don't clothe ourselves with Jesus, it is just like when we wear our filthy clothes. Friend, today we need to put on Jesus because the way Christians live their lives might be the only Bible others may read. Therefore, make sure you "clothe yourselves with the Lord Jesus Christ."

RESPONDER'S REFLECTION: If people can't see Jesus in our lives, the problem isn't with Jesus; instead, the problem is with us.

AUGUST 20TH

Proverbs 4:23 — "Above all else, guard your heart, for everything you do flows from it."

Be on guard! If a person is shot in the hand, leg, shoulder, or foot, they will most likely live through it. But if someone is shot through the heart, that person will probably die on the spot. This statement is not only true physically, but also spiritually as well. God wants us to guard our hearts from negative talk, complaining attitudes, and only focusing on the bad instead of the good. Be on guard and protect your heart!

RESPONDER'S REFLECTION: Many times, complaining can be contagious, but gratefulness can be contagious as well. What will you allow to grow in your heart?

AUGUST 21ST

1 Corinthians 1:25 — "For the foolishness of God is wiser than human wisdom, and the weakness of God is stronger than human strength."

The only way to receive God's power is to humble ourselves and fully depend upon him. Anytime we try to fix a problem on our own, we snatch the reins of our life out of God's hands and we place them back into ours. God desires for us to have his wisdom and strength, but we must give him the controls of our life today and every day! When we won't give control of our lives to God, it is a sign that pride is deep in our hearts.

RESPONDER'S REFLECTION: It doesn't take a lot of man if God has all the man. You can accomplish anything if you will empty yourself so Christ can fill you.

AUGUST 22ND

1 Corinthians 2:9 —"What no eye has seen, what no ear has heard, and what no human mind has conceived—the things God has prepared for those who love him."

Can you even imagine what heaven will be like? According to this verse, for those who put their faith in Christ, the things God has prepared for us after this life has ended will be awesome! I have heard it said many times that death is not the end, but the beginning! What a true and reassuring statement. Not only will heaven be incredible, but God also has amazing plans for us now! The key to experiencing what God has in store for us is to put our faith in Jesus. Trust God with your today, tomorrow, and eternity!

RESPONDER'S REFLECTION: For those whose faith is in Jesus, death is not the end but the beginning.

AUGUST 23RD

1 Corinthians 4:20 —"For the kingdom of God is not a matter of talk but of power."

Power is what we all need! Not the power affiliated with being rich or famous, but the power we need is more than that and only comes from God. We need God's power for many areas of our lives including to have strong marriages, to relate well with other people, to forgive others and ourselves, and to be healed on the inside. The good news is that God's power is available to us when we simply ask for it and are obedient to his will.

RESPONDER'S REFLECTION: Talk is cheap. People in our lives need to see and experience the real love and power of Jesus flowing out of us.

AUGUST 24TH

Proverbs 10:19 —"Sin is not ended by multiplying words, but the prudent hold their tongues."

This verse is a truth everyone needs to grasp and apply to his or her life. Today, when you are tempted to gossip, I want to encourage you to hold your tongue instead. If you have developed the habit of speaking negatively about your supervisor, consider staying quiet. If you struggle with complaining about others, think twice before doing so and choose instead to remain silent. Sometimes, speaking less is one of the best things we can do to bless our lives, but it can also be one of the most difficult things to do in life. Today, start practicing the art of holding your tongue.

RESPONDER'S REFLECTION: You can never unsay words. If you allow yourself to speak hurtful words to or about someone, you will never be able to take back those words. Choose your words wisely!

AUGUST 25TH

Proverbs 11:28 —"Those who trust in their riches will fall, but the righteous will thrive like a green leaf."

Money never made a man rich! I have never forgotten this expression when I heard it many years ago. When we trust in money, we fail every time. On the contrary, when we trust in God, we always succeed. God doesn't want your life just to be average, but he wants you to thrive. Today, if you are entrusting your life to money, a career, or anything other than God, realize that in order to thrive in life, you need put your trust in God alone!

RESPONDER'S REFLECTION: Money never made a man rich. Cars, houses, and toys are just material things that will eventually deteriorate. Put your trust in Jesus, not stuff.

AUGUST 26TH

Joshua 1:9 — "Do not be afraid; do not be discouraged."

Don't try to live without fear, but rather live through fear. Every single person on this planet will encounter fear at some point in his or her life. The important question is, will you go through it or be controlled by it? We can gain courage from the fact that the God of this universe is on our side and by our side. Bravery is not the absence of fear, but those who are brave are ready to face fear head-on and come out on top! The brave push forward through the fear.

RESPONDER'S REFLECTION: God wants you to live in faith, not in fear! What will you live in today?

AUGUST 27TH

Matthew 11:28—"Come to me, all you who are weary and burdened, and I will give you rest."

Jesus spoke these words approximately two thousand years ago and he continues to speak this same promise to you and me every day. Jesus wants us to come to him because we were not built to lug around the type of burdens and problems we often carry. As you start a new week, lighten your load by giving the burdens you are carrying to Jesus right now. If you try to carry the load that only Jesus can carry, you will wear yourself out. Take Jesus up on his promise to give you rest!

RESPONDER'S REFLECTION: Jesus Christ has all the power needed to carry every hurt, pain, and issue you may be facing. Exchange your burdens for his rest!

AUGUST 28TH

1 Corinthians 13:5 — "(Love) keeps no record of wrongs."

One of the many things I love about our Heavenly Father is that he chooses not to keep a record of our wrongs when we give our sins and mistakes to him. Since God isn't keeping a record of our sins, we need to also make sure we aren't keeping track of our own shortcomings. Furthermore, when our spouses, family, and friends have wronged us, we shouldn't keep a record of those mistakes either. When we love others, we should be able to overlook an offense just as Jesus does with us!

RESPONDER'S REFLECTION: A true sign that you love someone is you aren't keeping track of all that person's failures.

AUGUST 29TH

John 15:15 — "Instead, I have called you friends, for everything that I learned from my Father I have made known to you."

Have you ever considered this thought that God is not only your father, healer, and counselor, but he is also your friend? When we were born into this world, we didn't get to choose who our parents were going to be. Likewise, expecting parents don't get to pick out their kids. However, we do get to choose our friends. The fact that God is your friend shows an incredible truth that he picked you! The Almighty God of this world chose you and called you his friend.

RESPONDER'S REFLECTION: Isn't it comforting to know that God chose you to be his friend? When you start to understand this truth, you will soon realize how important and valued you are to God.

AUGUST 30TH

Romans 1:17 — "The righteous will live by faith."

It can be difficult for us to live by faith at times. Living by faith means that:

1. Even though you don't see an answer to the problem, you believe God has one.
2. You trust God even when you can't see him.
3. You don't give up on your dreams even when you have reason to do so.

Friend, God wants you to live by faith so that he can do more in and through your life than you ever imagined!

RESPONDER'S REFLECTION: You can't take a step of faith with God and play it safe. Living a life of faith means risk. However, there is tremendous reward and blessing with every risk.

AUGUST 31ST

Proverbs 20:22 — "Wait for the Lord, and he will avenge you."

Do you need God's help today? He will help you when you cry out to him. However, notice that the key to receiving help from God is not about us taking control of the situation, but instead waiting patiently for him to come to our aid. I once heard this phrase, "God is seldom early, but never late." He is a loving God who is always dependable. When we wait on God, we demonstrate through our actions that we trust him. Also, during this waiting period, we begin to develop deeper roots of spiritual maturity.

RESPONDER'S REFLECTION: God is seldom early, but never late. God and his promises are worth the wait!

SEPTEMBER 1ST

Micah 6:8 — "He has shown you, O mortal, what is good. And what does the Lord require of you? To act justly and to love mercy and to walk humbly with your God."

What is success in life? People have spent a lot of time, money, and energy trying to discover what it truly means to be successful. Some people erroneously believe they can find success in money, education, power, or fame. However, the answer can be found in today's scripture. According to Micah 6:8, focus your life on these three paths to be successful: act justly, love mercy, and walk humbly with God. God wants us to act right. God wants us to love right. God wants us to walk right.

RESPONDER'S REFLECTION: There is a difference between achievement and success. Achievement is about doing great things in our lives, whereas success is about doing great things in other people's lives!

SEPTEMBER 2ND

2 Corinthians 3:17 — "Where the Spirit of the Lord is, there is freedom."

God wants you to be free! He doesn't want you bound to low self-esteem, fear, sin, anxiety, depression, materialism, people pleasing, pain, or you name it. God only wants you bound to him and his love. Today, don't allow anyone or anything control your life that isn't from the Lord. Instead, invite the Spirit of the Lord into your life because only then will you experience true freedom!

RESPONDER'S REFLECTION: When you love someone, you give them freedom and choices. God is giving you the choice to have fear or faith, to be a victim or victor, or to live in bondage or freedom. Choose wisely!

SEPTEMBER 3RD

James 3:16 —"For where you have envy and selfish ambition, there you find disorder and every evil practice."

Nobody's success is robbing you of your potential! One of the worst things we can do is compare ourselves to others. When we make comparisons, the result is usually jealousy, insecurity, low self-confidence, and depression. Our lives can go sideways quickly when our unchecked flesh starts to covet what others have that we don't have. We need to celebrate and rejoice with others when they succeed, not come against them with feelings of envy and resentment.

RESPONDER'S REFLECTION: Nobody's success is robbing you of your potential! Celebrate with others when they succeed!

SEPTEMBER 4TH

2 Corinthians 6:16 —"As God has said: 'I will live with them and walk among them.'"

It is easy to make the comment, "May God be with you." However, the reality of the matter is that God is actually with us all the time. Look closer at this verse, "I will live with them and walk among them." Friend, it blows my mind how God promises to live with us and walk alongside us. I don't know about you, but I have experienced some crazy days in my journey through life. However, knowing that God is walking with me certainly encourages me to make it through those ups and downs of life.

RESPONDER'S REFLECTION: As your journey through life, be encouraged that you are not alone, because God lives and walks with you!

SEPTEMBER 5TH

Job 38:1 — "Then the Lord spoke to Job out of the storm."

You can't just trust the power of God, you must also trust the timing of God. God wants to speak to you and me during the worst storms of our lives! Everyone at times gets into a storm of anger, depression, unforgiveness, or pain. The Lord doesn't expect me to know it all, do it all, or own it all. However he desperately wants me to trust him through it all. You can make it through the storms of life! You can make it through the health issues! You can make it in spite of what is going on in your finances! You can make it through the relationship problems! God is speaking to you right now in spite of what is going on.

RESPONDER'S REFLECTION: The Lord doesn't expect me to know it all, do it all, or own it all. However he desperately wants me to trust him through it all! You can make it!

SEPTEMBER 6TH

Proverbs 26:12 — "Do you see a person wise in their own eyes? There is more hope for a fool than for them."

We all struggle with being prideful at times. Pride can permeate into your life when you begin to have success and then start to believe you can handle everything in your own strength. However, the truth is when we wake up each day, we need to humbly give everything to God and seek his wisdom and blessing. Today, if you are struggling in the area of pride, ask God to help you die to yourself and let him lead you instead. Pride will cause you to stumble and fall, so be sure to humble yourself before God today.

RESPONDER'S REFLECTION: You can't learn what you already know. We need to be humble and teachable, not prideful and arrogant.

SEPTEMBER 7TH

2 Corinthians 11:24-26 — "Five times I (Paul) received from the Jews the forty lashes minus one. Three times I was beaten with rods, once I was pelted with stones, three times I was shipwrecked...I have been constantly on the move. I have been in danger from rivers, in danger from bandits..."

After reading this verse, do you think you have it that bad? The Apostle Paul shares a list of hardships he encountered but that list doesn't even cover everything he experienced. Many times, if we are not careful, we can let the little things in life become something big. Don't allow the minor problems and issues you face today drag you down. Try not to make a mountain out of a molehill. Remember that you and God are a powerful team!

RESPONDER'S REFLECTION: When we focus too much attention on our problems, they appear to be huge. However, when we focus our attention on God, those same problems become smaller and insignificant.

SEPTEMBER 8TH

Psalm 118:24 — "The Lord has done it this very day; let us rejoice today and be glad."

Are you having a rough day? Join the crowd! We all have difficult days at times. However, we need to realize that God creates each new day for us to celebrate and enjoy. We should rejoice and be grateful to God for giving us this day! Delight in the truth that God loves you and rejoice because God has given you an amazing gift, which is today!

RESPONDER'S REFLECTION: Don't waste away your day complaining or worrying. Instead, rejoice in the Lord and make the most out of every opportunity he gives you today!

SEPTEMBER 9TH

Proverbs 30:5 — "Every word of God is flawless; he is a shield to those who take refuge in him."

Sometimes, the storms of life can batter and bruise you. If you are going through a storm today, take refuge in God. The word refuge means to be safe or sheltered from pursuit, danger, or trouble. God invites you to take refuge in him by coming in out of the rain and into his mercy, protection, and grace. He wants to shield you from any harm or danger that might come your way, but you need to receive his love and walk in relationship with him.

RESPONDER'S REFLECTION: The Word of God is flawless and is our perfect shield, guide, counselor, and source of nourishment for our soul.

SEPTEMBER 10TH

Romans 1:25 — "They exchanged the truth about God for a lie."

Many times, we act upon this scripture without even realizing it. The truth is…we can rebound from any mistake, but sometimes we believe the lie that all is lost. The truth is…God can heal any relationship in our life, but sometimes we believe the lie that our relationships can never be restored. The truth is…we can do all things through Christ, but sometimes we believe the lie that we have limits on our lives. Friend, if you have exchanged the truth about God for a lie, it is time to exchange that lie for the truth!

RESPONDER'S REFLECTION: The truth sets people free, but the truth only has power if it is believed!

SEPTEMBER 11TH

Galatians 1:23 —"They only heard the report: The man who formerly perse-cuted us (the church) is now preaching the faith he once tried to destroy."

God can use your greatest pain as a platform for his power and glory. God is in the business of turning lives around for his glory! Regardless of the failures or mistakes we have made, God is able to turn it around for good. We can never lose sight of this fact that God specializes in accomplishing what humankind thinks is impossible. Friend, if there is an area of your life you want God to turn around, he will do it if you give it to him. Isn't that good news?

RESPONDER'S REFLECTION: God can use our greatest pain as a plat-form for his power and glory to be expressed in our lives.

SEPTEMBER 12TH

Psalm 2:2 —"The kings of the earth rise up and the rulers band together against the Lord."

Psalm 2:4 —"The One enthroned in heaven laughs; the Lord scoffs at them."

This passage of scripture actually shows God laughing when his enemies try to come against him. This situation hardly seems like a laughing matter, but God can laugh because he is all-powerful and there is not one thing or person who can defeat him. Understanding this truth about God, should give us reassurance that God can handle any trial we encounter. The worst thing that can happen to us as believers in Jesus is we die. Then afterwards, we get to spend eternity in heaven! Therefore, whatever hardships you are facing, know that God is so much bigger than that issue.

RESPONDER'S REFLECTION: God is able to laugh when anyone or any-thing tries to come against him because he is Almighty God. He is and will always be victorious, and he gives us the victory to overcome any trial we may face today!

SEPTEMBER 13TH

Psalm 3:3 —"But you, Lord, are a shield around me, my glory, the One who lifts my head high."

What thoughts come to mind when you reflect on this truth that the Lord is a shield around you? A shield encloses and protects one from risk or danger. When God is our shield, it means he is with us completely and will enclose and keep us safe from harm. In the truest form, God hems us in behind, before, and all around! What an amazing God we serve. Today, remember that God always has your back!

RESPONDER'S REFLECTION: When God is for you, there isn't a devil in hell that can stop you! God is your shield and protection.

SEPTEMBER 14TH

Psalm 92:4 —"For you make me glad by your deeds, Lord; I sing for joy at what your hands have done."

God does so much for us! However, the one instance in which God's hands are tied where he can't do anything for us occurs if we decide to quit. God is not able to bless your job, marriage, or anything else if you decide to give up and quit. Are you tempted to quit on your dream, spouse, child, business opportunity, church, or life in general? Friend, if you decide to throw in the towel, then you will stop receiving all that God has for you to change the situation you are experiencing. Hang in there and don't quit!

RESPONDER'S REFLECTION: As a child of God, you can't be defeated if you will refuse to quit. Keep going and don't give up!

SEPTEMBER 15TH

Psalm 7:8—"Let the Lord judge the peoples."

The more we judge people, the more problems that will occur in our relationships. It seems as though when we judge others, we always come out on the losing end. We need to come to the conclusion that the more we take our eyes off of people and put our eyes on God, the more blessed we will be. I want to encourage you to love and pray for the people you disagree with, but don't judge them. Focus on being the best you can be, and let God take care of the rest.

RESPONDER'S REFLECTION: When we start judging people, we have taken a turn down the wrong path that will only lead to destruction.

SEPTEMBER 16TH

Ephesians 3:20 —"Now to him who is able to do immeasurably more than all we ask or imagine, according to his power that is at work within us."

God is a God of more than enough! Today, we read a promise that expresses how God is able to do immeasurably more than all we ask or imagine… Wow! Notice that we can't even begin to measure the power of God because it is beyond our comprehension. I don't know which is more difficult to understand — God's power or his desire to use his power on our behalf! We serve such an awesome God!

RESPONDER'S REFLECTION: God wants to display his power in your life by doing more than you could ever imagine! Don't listen to the devil who will lie and tell you differently.

SEPTEMBER 17TH

Philippians 4:13 —"I can do all this through him who gives me strength."

Do you struggle with believing you can do all things? Are you saying the words, "I can't" when God is saying, "You can"? Friend, God wants you to know today that "You can!" The key to being able to do all things is you must live through Christ. If you are facing all your tasks through Christ and in his strength, then you can do all things! Where you start to get into trouble is when you attempt to do all things through yourself and in your own strength. The truth is we can only be successful when we move in God's strength and allow him to remove any limits on our life.

RESPONDER'S REFLECTION: Are you saying, "I can't" when God is saying, "You can." Today, God wants you to know "You can!"

SEPTEMBER 18TH

Psalm 12:6 —"And the words of the Lord are flawless."

It sure would be great if we lived in a world that was flawless, but unfortunately, this isn't the case! It doesn't matter how well a house is built, it will eventually deteriorate. Regardless of which political party is in office at the time, our country will never be perfect. After you buy your dream car, it will depreciate and break down at some point. Nothing in this world is flawless, except for the Word of God. The Bible is God's perfect road map, which makes it easier to live in this imperfect world, but we just need to make sure we use it!

RESPONDER'S REFLECTION: We live in a broken and imperfect world. However, God does give us the perfect GPS, which is his Word. Hide God's Word in your heart today!

SEPTEMBER 19TH

Psalm 13:5-6 — "But I trust in your unfailing love; my heart rejoices in your salvation. I will sing the Lord's praise, for he has been good to me."

God's love never fails. There will be days when you are able to rejoice on the mountaintops of victories in your life and then on other days, you may have to suffer in the dark valleys of loss and pain. However, God always has his good purposes in mind. Your pain can become God's platform. God wants to use the dark times of our lives just like he wants to use the best times in our lives. The love of God is not achieved it is received. God's love for you today is so much bigger than you can even imagine.

RESPONDER'S REFLECTION: We can't completely measure the goodness of God in this life alone. God has been so good to us in many ways that we won't fully see or understand them until we are with him in heaven. God's love can't be achieved it can only be received.

SEPTEMBER 20TH

Joshua 21:45 — "Not one of all the Lord's good promises to Israel failed; every one was fulfilled."

Wow, this verse has some incredible news! Every promise God makes, he fulfills which includes forgiving all our sins, healing our lives, giving us peace, renewing our strength, and so much more! Friend, the Bible is packed with God's promises and the good news is that God is batting one thousand. If you think God is taking longer than you would like to fulfill his promises to you, don't stop believing. He is faithful and will always come through on his promises!

RESPONDER'S REFLECTION: Too many times, we try to put a time limit on God, and the only thing that will do is get us frustrated. God knows what we need and when we need it. Rest in his perfect timing!

SEPTEMBER 21ST

Psalm 121:1-2 —"I lift my eyes to the mountains—where does my help come from? My help comes from the Lord, the Maker of heaven and earth."

Where do you turn to get the strength and help you need during the tough times of life? If you trust in anything or anyone other than the Lord, you can bet your bottom dollar you won't receive the strength you need to make it through life. Today, lift your eyes to the Lord for strength. If he created heaven and Earth, he can create an answer for anything life throws at you.

RESPONDER'S REFLECTION: Get your hopes up! There are times when others may tell you the opposite to try to protect you from being disappointed. Friend, as children of God we need to get our hopes up because we serve a limitless, Almighty God.

SEPTEMBER 22ND

Lamentations 3:22-23 —"For his compassions never fail. They are new every morning."

This verse gives us a great promise that God's compassion and mercy toward us are new every morning. Why is this good news? Because, regardless of who we are, there will be times when we mess things up in our finances, marriage, and personal matters. However, when we fall short and go to God, he extends his fresh grace and mercy to us each day. Consequently, if you have slipped up recently, don't forget that God's mercies toward you are new this morning.

RESPONDER'S REFLECTION: Today is a brand new start for you! Yesterday is history, tomorrow is a mystery, but thank God, you have today.

SEPTEMBER 23RD

Romans 8:1 —"Therefore, there is now no condemnation for those who are in Christ Jesus."

As you read today's verse, realize that God doesn't want you feeling guilty for your sins and mistakes after you have given them to him and repented. It is healthy to feel conviction when you sin, but once you confess your sin to God and ask him to forgive you; he will free you from sin so you can experience life with him. The devil wants you always feeling guilty and condemned by getting you to focus on every mistake you have made. On the contrary, God wants you to know that he has paid the price for every sin so you can walk in freedom!

RESPONDER'S REFLECTION: The grace of God isn't just a promise offered for the future, but is for today as well. Right now, God wants to exchange your guilt for his peace.

SEPTEMBER 24TH

Galatians 4:7 —"So you are no longer a slave, but God's child."

It is not only important to remember who you are; it is important to remember whose you are. Sometimes, people struggle in life because they have the wrong picture of God. They might think God is sitting in heaven waiting to strike them down with lightning bolts every time they make a mistake. Or, as the above verse mentions, some people think they are God's slaves. However, both pictures are inaccurate. For those who have put their faith in Christ, you are not a slave, but a son or daughter of God's. No matter how many times I have messed up, I will always be the son of my dad, Tom Young. In the same way, you are not perfect and will make mistakes at times, but that doesn't mean you are no longer a son or daughter of God. Be blessed, and don't forget you are a King's kid!

RESPONDER'S REFLECTION: It is not only important to remember who you are; it is important to remember whose you are.

SEPTEMBER 25TH

2 Corinthians 5:7 —"For we live by faith, not by sight."

We need to keep this truth in our hearts and minds every day! Why? Because the devil will try to get us discouraged by what we see. Friend, if we spend too much time focused on all the problems in this world, we will become disheartened and depressed. However, if our hope and focus are on Christ, we can overcome what we perceive to be a problem and gain the victory. Try not to view a hardship as a problem, but instead view it as an opportunity for God to show his power!

RESPONDER'S REFLECTION: If you live your life walking by sight, you will never accomplish the impossible. If you want to live a life that changes the world, you must walk by faith.

SEPTEMBER 26TH

2 Corinthians 6:10 —"Having nothing, and yet possessing everything."

The only way this verse can be true is when God is involved. You could be struggling with your finances, but with God, still be rich in life. You could be dealing with health issues, but with God, still have wholeness in your heart. You could be afraid, but with God, still have confidence to take down a giant you are facing. All things could be going wrong in life, but with God, you still have peace in the depths of your soul. The best of this life can only happen with God!

RESPONDER'S REFLECTION: When God is involved, we possess everything we need to be successful in this life!

SEPTEMBER 27TH

Judges 6:23 — "But the Lord said to him, 'Peace! Do not be afraid. You are not going to die.'"

Have you ever thought something dreadful was going to happen, only to find out it didn't? Maybe you thought you wouldn't be paid, or you would lose your job, or the plane you were on might crash. The devil specializes in trying to deceive us through the lies he tells about the situations in our lives. Today, receive God's truth, which is "Peace! Do not be afraid." God wants you to have his peace and to live a life free from fear and anxiety.

RESPONDER'S REFLECTION: Many of the scary thoughts and imaginations that race into our minds typically don't happen. Don't listen to the lies of the devil; rest in God's peace instead.

SEPTEMBER 28TH

Psalm 103:3 — "(God) heals all our diseases."

Many times, when we read this verse, we think it refers to God's power to heal only the physical body. However, God not only heals the physical, but he also heals wounded hearts and souls. Today, if you are struggling with fear, anxiety, depression, guilt, stress, loneliness, or heartbreak, the good news is that God heals *all* areas. It is powerful to know that God promises to heal our souls and emotions because there is no x-ray that can reveal what is wrong inside our souls. God sees everything and he is the perfect healer.

RESPONDER'S REFLECTION: God is able to heal all areas of our lives, the physical as well as our broken hearts. What part of *all* do we sometimes not understand?

SEPTEMBER 29TH

2 Corinthians 10:5 —"We take captive every thought to make it obedient to Christ."

The powerful expression about the battlefield being in our mind is so true! Unfortunately, our thoughts can wreak havoc on our lives. Sometimes, we think we can't do something, so then we can't do it. Or, we might think we are going to fail, so we fail. Today, God wants you to discard any thought you have about yourself as a failure, loser, or underachiever. He wants you to get rid of anxious, stressful, sinful, and painful thoughts. At times, we all will struggle with having negative thoughts. However, the way we change that kind of thinking is by replacing those thoughts with the power and love of God's Word.

RESPONDER'S REFLECTION: The key to removing negative thoughts is by replacing them with God's Word. When you change your thinking, you change your life.

SEPTEMBER 30TH

Psalm 55:22 — "Cast your cares on the Lord and he will sustain you."

Most of us understand that God loves us, but how often do we consider that he genuinely cares about our every need? He is not only concerned about the larger trials that occur in our lives, but he also pays attention to the minor issues as well. My pastor growing up once said, "If something bothers you, it bothers God." Friend, God loves you so much that he is concerned about all of your cares, even the smaller ones. As you go through this day, be sure to cast all your cares, whether large or small, on the Lord. Don't hold onto the burdens that God is willing to carry for you.

RESPONDER'S REFLECTION: God is genuinely concerned about you. If something bothers you, it bothers God.

OCTOBER 1ST

John 11:35 —"Jesus wept."

Jesus was and still is a model of compassion. Today, he weeps when his children experience loss. He weeps at funerals. He weeps in divorce court. He weeps in prison. This is our God. He's not detached from our problems and the realities we face. He's a God who understands our suffering, and he strengthens us to bear the pain we experience at times in this life.

RESPONDER'S REFLECTION: Jesus is moved with compassion by what is going on in your life. He understands what you are suffering and will walk through it with you!

OCTOBER 2ND

1 John 4:16 —"And so we know and rely on the love God has for us."

The love of God is infinite. He does not ration out his love, but if we want to experience more of it, we need to come to him with an expectant heart. Spend time in God's presence asking him to pour out his love in your marriage, family, friendships, and every area of your life. The love of God is the answer to any problem you encounter. C.S. Lewis once said, "Though our feelings come and go, God's love for us does not." When you face trials in life, be sure to rely on the everlasting love of God!

RESPONDER'S REFLECTION: Though trials and issues in life will come and go, the love of God will always remain with us.

OCTOBER 3RD

Psalm 29:10 — "The Lord is enthroned as King forever."

You can't turn the TV on during election time without seeing numerous political campaign ads. Each commercial shows different candidates making promises of how they will change this nation and American lives for the better. However, most times, those promises are broken and not fulfilled. On the contrary, God is enthroned as King forever and not only does he keep all of his promises, but he will never be voted out! As you go through your day, remember that God is in control, not political leaders, supervisors, family, or friends. Only God is in charge, and he is for us!

RESPONDER'S REFLECTION: God is our King, and our job is to listen to and obey him. We will be disappointed if we let anyone else be in control of our lives other than God.

OCTOBER 4TH

Psalm 29:11 — "The Lord gives strength to his people."

Do you need more strength today? I am not referring to strength in your physical body, but more for your mind, soul, and emotions. If you are in need of that kind of strength, make sure you go to the correct source. You won't find what you are looking for from the latest fad, self-help book, or motivational speech. No, the strength you need only comes from God. The Lord is giving out his strength, so make sure you are in a position to receive from him today!

RESPONDER'S REFLECTION: Jesus displays his power in your life only in your weakness. God will give you the strength you need during the weaknesses and trials of life.

OCTOBER 5TH

Romans 8:38-39 — "For I am convinced that neither death nor life, neither angels nor demons, neither the present nor the future, nor any powers, neither height not depth, nor anything else in all creation, will be able to separate us from the love of God that is in Christ Jesus our Lord."

Today's verses make it abundantly clear that God's love is steady, unchanging, and unbreakable! No exceptions are made when referring to the steadfast love of God because absolutely nothing can separate a Christian from God's love — not performance, not bad circumstances, not anything! There is no failure on our part, no attack on the devil's part, and no accusation on someone else's part that can separate us from God's love. Isn't that amazing news?

RESPONDER'S REFLECTION: Your performance does not change how much God loves you. Because of the powerful work that Jesus did on the cross, nothing can keep God from loving you.

OCTOBER 6TH

Psalm 31:24 — "Be strong and take heart, all you who hope in the Lord."

God wants you to be strong in him and have the power to overcome any problems you might be having with your co-workers, family, thought life, or anything else that is dragging you down. The key to receiving God's power is to take your eyes off the problem and put them on the answer, Jesus Christ. Friend, if your hope is in the Lord, you will be strong to face any of the issues that life throws your way.

RESPONDER'S REFLECTION: We can be strong because the death and resurrection of Jesus has made the devil powerless! The only thing the devil can try to do is tell you lies. Don't believe him!

OCTOBER 7TH

Psalm 32:10 —"The Lord's unfailing love surrounds the one who trusts in him."

The expression, "You're surrounded!" isn't good news if you have broken the law and you are hearing this announcement from the police. However, when God is the one making this same statement, it is great news! God wants you to know "you're surrounded" by his unfailing love. Today is a good day because when you put your hope and trust in God, he will surround you in his love and protection.

RESPONDER'S REFLECTION: When the love of God surrounds you, there is nothing to fear in life!

OCTOBER 8TH

Psalm 32:5 —"I will confess my transgressions to the Lord. And you forgave the guilt of my sin."

God declares us innocent when we confess our sins and mistakes to him. Most people understand that God will forgive their sins, but they still might struggle with feelings of guilt associated with those wrongdoings. However, the truth is that after you have repented of your sins to God, he not only forgives you, but he also removes guilt. Because of the sacrifice Jesus made on the cross, you no longer have to feel guilty!

RESPONDER'S REFLECTION: The blood of Jesus not only covers your sins and gives you mercy, but God also declares you innocent. Don't try to pay a debt that God has already paid in full.

OCTOBER 9TH

1 Timothy 6:6 — "But godliness with contentment is great gain."

Don't let what you don't have keep you from being thankful for what you do have. The devil does not want you to be content! The devil always wants you unfulfilled! Don't focus on what you don't have, focus on what you do have. Don't look at the time you lost, look at the time you have. Don't consider the opportunities you missed, consider the opportunities that are approaching. Today is the perfect day for a supernatural breakthrough in your life! The moment you walk with Jesus and become content in life, is the very moment you position yourself for everything God has planned for you.

RESPONDER'S REFLECTION: Don't let what you don't have keep you from being thankful for what you do have. If you have Jesus, you have everything!

OCTOBER 10TH

Matthew 6:25 — "Therefore I tell you, do not worry."

Wow, what a command! Jesus tells us not to worry or to state it differently, not to be stressed out! You might be thinking that this concept of not worrying is easier said than done, and you are probably correct. However, we can get rid of a lot of our worry and stress by trusting God with every detail of what is going on in our lives. Today, give God every issue that is causing you stress and anxiety. When God is taking care of everything, you don't need to worry because your life is in the best hands!

RESPONDER'S REFLECTION: Worry is the opposite of trust. Worry is oftentimes an indicator that we are struggling to submit an area of our life to God and trust him.

OCTOBER 11TH

Ephesians 3:20 — "Now to him who is able to do immeasurably more than all we ask or imagine, according to his power that is at work within us."

What do you need God to do in your life? Do you need a fresh vision? Do you need healing in a relationship with a family member or friend? Is there a person in your life you can't forgive? Has someone or something hurt you? Are the demands of your job causing you a lot of stress? Friend, if you answered yes to one or more of those questions, the good news is God "is able to do immeasurably more than all we ask or imagine." Get your hopes up and watch how the Lord will move on your behalf!

RESPONDER'S REFLECTION: God can do more than we imagine! Make sure you are not putting up barriers of doubt that stand in your way of having all God wants for you.

OCTOBER 12TH

Psalm 147:3 — "He heals the brokenhearted and binds up their wounds."

Don't become who hurt you. Often when someone grows up in a negative home when they become adults they become negative. We have seen those that are sexually abused become abusers of others. All of us have experienced hurts through people or painful situations. However, many times what hurts us soon becomes who we are. Don't let this happen! Flip the script on the person or problem that hurt you. The moment you start returning good for evil is the moment your supernatural breakthrough and emotional healing start to take place. There is always a divine appointment on the other side of a disappointment.

RESPONDER'S REFLECTION: Don't become who hurt you. There is always a divine appointment on the other side of a disappointment.

OCTOBER 13TH

Colossians 3:2 — "Set your minds on things above, not on earthly things."

Oftentimes, what we set our minds on will determine the course and direction for our life. In addition, what we think about most is a barometer of what we value and deem as most important in our lives. Many times, if we are honest, we can spend too much time only thinking about ourselves. However, if you only think about you all the time, you will be miserable. On the contrary, when you focus your mind on God and others before your own needs, only then can you experience a fulfilling, abundant life.

RESPONDER'S REFLECTION: What you think about the most determines what you deem as most important in your life.

OCTOBER 14TH

Psalm 39:5 — "Everyone is but a breath."

Stop wasting time! The Bible states in today's verse, "Everyone is but a breath." Today, don't waste your life being disconnected and estranged from your loved ones. Today, forgive those who have hurt you even if they haven't asked for your forgiveness. Today, make a choice to live each day as if it was your last. Today, don't give into fear, but believe God's promises for your life. Today, don't hold on to the pain of the past. Even if you live into your 90s, your life is still short compared to eternity, so live each day to its fullest!

RESPONDER'S REFLECTION: Don't be a yesterday person. Don't be a tomorrow person. Be a today person!

OCTOBER 15TH

Psalm 130:1 —"Out of the depths I cry to you, Lord."

Why was the writer of this Psalm crying to God from the depths of his soul? Because he knew God would listen! You don't have to be perfect or have your life in order for God to hear your prayers. In fact, the opposite is true! We tend to cry to God during our worst and darkest times in life. God is listening and hears our hearts when we cry out to him. Friend, if you are in the depths of stress, guilt, sin, pain, or depression, the good news is that God is listening, so cry out to him today!

RESPONDER'S REFLECTION: While we may view the issues or pain we face as valleys, God views them as a platform to take us places we have never been before.

OCTOBER 16TH

Philippians 3:13 —"Forgetting what is behind and straining toward what is ahead."

You can't reach your destiny if you are living in your history! The devil wants to trap you in your past. Whether you are living in a happy or sad past, God wants you to come out of the past. I thank God for past victories but if you are still living in those, you will never have victories today. Perhaps you are bound to the past by guilt, sins, or mistakes. Jesus Christ died to break those chains. Come out of the past today. God wants to do miraculous, amazing, supernatural exploits in your life today!

RESPONDER'S REFLECTION: You can't reach your destiny if you're living in your history!

OCTOBER 17TH

Psalm 43:5 —"Put your hope in God."

Have you ever opened a Christmas or birthday present and been disappointed by what you found inside? I think we have all had that experience at some point in our life. However, with God, we can put our hope in him because he will never disappoint us. In fact, he is the God of more than enough! Don't make the mistake of putting your hope in anything created by God; instead, put your hope in the Creator.

RESPONDER'S REFLECTION: Disappointment is a feeling of dissatisfaction that occurs when your expectations are not met. With God, he will never disappoint, so put your hope in him today!

OCTOBER 18TH

Psalm 46:10 —"Be still, and know that I am God."

This verse about being still can be difficult to apply to our lives. There are times when God speaks loudly and other times, quietly. In order to hear what God is saying, we often need to turn down the volume of this world and its demands. For example, we may have to turn off the news, or take a break from social media, or unplug from our smartphones and answering emails. If we don't disconnect from the distractions of this world, we run the risk of missing what God is trying to say to us.

RESPONDER'S REFLECTION: God doesn't want to be part of your multitasking. He wants your undivided attention. Be still and listen when God speaks to you.

OCTOBER 19TH

Psalm 46:1 — "God is our refuge and strength."

You are a warrior! You are powerful! You can't be defeated! You are a conqueror! You are a victor! All these statements are true as long as you look to God for your strength. (See Romans 8:28, Philippians 4:13, and Proverbs 16:3.) I once heard Joyce Meyer say, "You can either be pitiful or powerful, but you can't be both." When you try to be strong without God, you will grow weak. God wants you to be powerful in him today.

RESPONDER'S REFLECTION: If you want more supernatural authority in your life, stop repeating the lies the devil says about you, and start repeating what God says about you.

OCTOBER 20TH

Psalm 105:1 — "Give praise to the Lord, proclaim his name."

Ernie Harwell was the voice of the Detroit Tigers for over 40 years. When inducted into the Baseball Hall of Fame he said, "I praise the Lord here today. I know that all my talent and all my ability comes from him, and without him I'm nothing and I thank him for his great blessing." When we praise God and give him the glory, the limits on our lives are removed. When we sing our own praises, we put a lid on how much can be accomplished in our lives. Today, remember to give God all the honor and glory because he deserves it!

RESPONDER'S REFLECTION: When we accept the credit for what God has done in and through our lives, we are actually stealing God's glory.

OCTOBER 21ST

James 2:23 — "Abraham believed God, and it was credited to him as righteousness, and he was called God's friend."

When expecting parents give birth, they usually accept and love the child who is born to them. What is the point? We can't choose family, but we get to choose our friends. The love of God is incredible because he chose us! For those who have put their faith in Jesus, God not only loves us as his children, but he takes it a step further and calls us his friends. Today, don't forget that God is not only your Heavenly Father, but also your friend!

RESPONDER'S REFLECTION: Before you were born, God saw every mistake you would ever make and he still chose you. Today, understand how precious and valued you are to God because he calls you his friend.

OCTOBER 22ND

Psalm 95:2 — "Let us come before him with thanksgiving and extol him with music and song."

To be honest, the world we live in can be a rough and dangerous place. There is so much violence, pain, hurt, and brokenness that can overwhelm people at times. However, despite all the evil and corruption in our society, there is still so much to thank God for in our lives. Friend, I want to encourage you to make the choice to be thankful in all situations you encounter. Secondly, discover opportunities to serve and help those who may have less reasons to be thankful than you.

RESPONDER'S REFLECTION: We have numerous reasons to thank and praise God. Today, spend time thinking about and possibly writing down those things for which you are thankful. Also, look for opportunities to help those who have less reasons to be thankful than you.

OCTOBER 23RD

Psalm 52:8 —"But I am like an olive tree flourishing in the house of God; I trust in God's unfailing love for ever and ever."

Are you flourishing in life? If you can't answer "yes" to this question, the reason can be boiled down to one truth, which is difficulty trusting God. At times, we all struggle with fully relying and depending on God. Trusting is sometimes easier said than done, but two things should make it easier: First, understand that God's love for you is unfailing even when you fail him and secondly, recognize that when you trust God, you will flourish.

RESPONDER'S REFLECTION: To flourish in life, you must rid your life of selfishness and fear, and place your trust in God's unfailing love.

OCTOBER 24TH

John 15:19 —"But I have chosen you out of the world."

Why do people struggle with low self-esteem? Some might suggest that the harsh words others have spoken or certain physical/emotional short-comings are the main culprits for low self-esteem. However, I believe self-esteem issues stem from people either not knowing or believing what God says about them. In today's verse, God states, "I have chosen you." Friend, regardless of any physical imperfections you think you have with your height or weight, God chose you. Despite what others might say or think about you, God chose you. The bottom line is that you are extremely important to God! If you are struggling with low self-esteem, listen to God and what his Word says about you because he chose you!

RESPONDER'S REFLECTION: What determines the value of an object is what the owner is willing to pay for it. God loves and values you so much that he was willing to pay with the sacrifice of his own son just for you!

OCTOBER 25TH

1 Samuel 12:11 — "He (God) delivered you from the hands of your enemies all around you, so that you lived in safety."

Overwhelmed is a word Americans often use to describe how they feel. However, for those whose faith is in Christ, we should feel the exact opposite. Why? Because God's Word gives us a promise that even when we feel like the problems of life are surrounding us, he will deliver us so that we can live in safety. If you feel overwhelmed today, resist those feelings. Feed your faith, and doubt your doubts.

RESPONDER'S REFLECTION: Today, you can choose to feed anxiety or faith. Choose wisely, because what you feed will grow.

OCTOBER 26TH

2 Thessalonians 3:4 — "We have confidence in the Lord."

Putting our confidence in the Lord is simple when the big paychecks are rolling in, when the kids are behaving, and when things are going smoothly at the job. However, we not only need to have confidence in the Lord when times are good, but we need even more confidence in God during our difficult and dark days. Friend, God is faithful to follow through on all his promises for our lives. Today, get excited and know that when your confidence is in the Lord, you can't be defeated!

RESPONDER'S REFLECTION: When your confidence is in God, you will be a champion in life!

OCTOBER 27TH

Judges 16:28 —"Please, God, strengthen me just once more."

Today's verse is Samson's prayer after he had failed God, and before he achieved his greatest victory. What is the point? The fact is when we fail God, it doesn't mean he is finished with us. No matter who you are, there will be times when you fall short and fail God just as Samson did. However, the ultimate failure is if we choose to give up. Samson didn't give up and God used him the most after he blew it. He can do the same with us.

RESPONDER'S REFLECTION: God wants to turn your failures around for good to bring him glory. Many people in your sphere of influence need to see the testimony of God in your life!

OCTOBER 28TH

Deuteronomy 31:8 —"The Lord himself goes before you and will be with you."

These six words can bring you comfort, "The Lord himself goes before you." Regardless of whether you are experiencing joy and favor or stressful and painful times, God goes before you to pave the way. As a result, he can give you guidance on how to maneuver around life's biggest pits and problems. Today, you can have peace in knowing that God is always one-step ahead guiding and preparing your steps to overcome any problem that might be on the horizon.

RESPONDER'S REFLECTION: If the Lord has gone before you, he knows exactly how to guide you through all of the zigs and zags of life.

OCTOBER 29TH

Psalm 121:1 — "I lift up my eyes."

Wherever you focus your eyes typically is where you walk or drive. Well the same is true in life. If you are always looking down at your problems, looking down in shame, looking down in guilt, looking down in worry, then that is where your life will be. However, God wants you to lift your eyes off your problems and onto him! Get your focus off the pain and past issues of life.

RESPONDER'S REFLECTION: In order to be effective with a firearm you have to focus on the target. The devil wants your focus down and God wants your focus up. If something negative has your focus down, kick it to the curb.

OCTOBER 30TH

Psalm 60:12 — "With God we will gain the victory."

God wants you to have victory in your life! However, notice that victory doesn't just happen automatically. The key words in this verse are "With God." In order to gain victory, you must partner with God. If you haven't invited God into your life, marriage, finances, and relationships, I encourage you to do so today so that you will have the victory!

RESPONDER'S REFLECTION: If you want to have everything in life that God wants you to have, the devil will fight you for it. However, the devil is now a powerless opponent because Jesus died on the cross and rose from the grave and we have gained the victory!

OCTOBER 31ST

Psalm 62:8 — "Pour out your hearts to him, for God is our refuge."

Have you ever suppressed feelings of anger, bitterness, or resentment to the point where you just couldn't handle it any longer? Don't blow your top! Instead, I want to encourage you to apply this verse to your life by pouring out your hearts to God. When you share all your struggles and secrets with God, he is the only one whose advice is one hundred percent accurate, and who understands exactly what you are going through. Don't burden your family and friends with the problems only God can carry. Unload your troubles at the feet of Jesus.

RESPONDER'S REFLECTION: The Lord Jesus himself carried our sins and burdens to the cross. Don't take back what Jesus has gladly taken from you.

NOVEMBER 1ST

1 John 1:3 — "And our fellowship is with the Father and with his Son, Jesus Christ."

Fellowship defined means *communion or intimacy.* God desires to have fellowship with us. Many times, we treat God as if he is a genie in a bottle where we make one request after another to him. Even though God is our provider and he gladly listens to our requests, he yearns for us to have a deeper, more intimate relationship with him. Today, if you haven't already done so, begin talking with God and listening to him with the understanding that he desires fellowship and friendship with you!

RESPONDER'S REFLECTION: God desires to have fellowship with you. Make it your goal to spend time with God daily. Meeting alone with God is a privilege, not an obligation!

NOVEMBER 2ND

Psalm 63:7 — "You are my help."

We all have hurts, habits, and hang-ups in our lives. The difference between those who overcome trials and those who don't is simply that those who prevail know where to turn for help. Today, in your largest or even smallest of trials, turn to God because he wants to be your help. Remember that with God's aid, you will be an overcomer instead of being overcome by the troubles you face.

RESPONDER'S REFLECTION: If you want to have victory in life, remember to turn to God for help! If you do, you will be a winner every time!

NOVEMBER 3RD

Hebrews 11:6 — "And without faith it is impossible to please God, because anyone who comes to him must believe that he exists and that he rewards those who earnestly seek him."

Are you struggling with your faith in God? The devil wants you to think about every reason why you shouldn't trust God. However, the best things in life require faith. When you get married, you have faith in your spouse and give them love. When you become parents, you have faith in your children to follow you and make good choices. We, along with our spouses and kids can't be perfect, but God is and that is why we should place our faith in him. No matter what you are going through today, have faith and believe that God will move on your behalf because he loves you!

RESPONDER'S REFLECTION: Faith is an action that will require risk. Step out today and trust God. Don't trust what you see trust what you know.

NOVEMBER 4TH

Philippians 4:13 —"I can do all this through him who gives me strength."

Are you limiting God from working in your life? Some examples of ways we can limit God are being negative, unforgiving, or doubting his love and power. This verse promises that, "I can do all this through him." In other words, if you will partner with God and let him be in full control, all limits will be removed where God can do the impossible through your life. Oftentimes, we want God's power, but we want our will to be done. However, in order to have God's power, you must submit to his will.

RESPONDER'S REFLECTION: If you struggle with surrendering your will to God, the root issue could be that you don't really understand how good God's plans are for you.

NOVEMBER 5TH

Proverbs 18:21 —"The tongue has the power of life and death."

Don't let your words become your prison! If you speak negativity over your relationships, job, finances, and family, you will reap negativity. When you are in a tough spot and start complaining, your grumbling won't make that situation any better. Remember, you can't sow one thing and reap another. For example, if you sow words of anger and hate, don't expect to reap love and kindness. Whatever you sow with your words, you are going to reap in your life. Regardless of what you are facing or who is around you, don't sow harmful things with your words. Instead, speak the word of God over every situation you face, and you will reap good things.

RESPONDER'S REFLECTION: That law of sowing and reaping is in effect on every person's life. Sow what you want to reap.

NOVEMBER 6TH

Psalm 96:3 — "Declare his glory."

If you want more of God's authority in your life, declare what he says about you. Almost every morning, I declare and agree with what God's Word says about me. I daily proclaim that I am saved (Romans 10:13), forgiven (1 John 1:9), victorious (Luke 1:37), healed (Isaiah 53:5), prosperous (Malachi 3:10), protected (Psalm 91:11), and at peace (Isaiah 26:3). Today, read God's Word and agree with what he says about you!

RESPONDER'S REFLECTION: Standing on the promises of man will leave you unfulfilled, while standing on the promises of God will leave you fully satisfied!

NOVEMBER 7TH

Psalm 40:10 — "I speak of your faithfulness and your saving help."

Have you ever needed saving from yourself? Maybe, you said something that you later regretted, or you made a promise you couldn't keep. Perhaps you made a financial commitment, but later realized your budget couldn't handle it. Friend, God has the power not only to give us eternal life, but also to save us from the predicaments we get ourselves into from time to time. If you are in a jam, stop fighting and start looking up to God.

RESPONDER'S REFLECTION: The majority of the problems we face, we actually cause ourselves. Healthy choices lead to healthy lives and those kinds of choices can only come from listening to the heart of God.

NOVEMBER 8TH

Psalm 71:14 —"As for me, I will always have hope."

Today is a new day, which means it is back to work, back to school, back to retirement, or just back to life. God knows before you do what issues you are going to face today. However, he wants you to understand that regardless of the good or bad that might come your way, you can "always have hope." Why is this statement true? Because God is not caught off-guard or surprised by what you encounter today. When you experience the trials and pushbacks of life, God has already gone before you and will lead you through those difficulties. God knows what lies ahead, so you can have hope because your guide is God. Let the guidance of God direct your steps today.

RESPONDER'S REFLECTION: Our guide through life is our loving God!

NOVEMBER 9TH

Hebrews 6:15 —"After waiting patiently, Abraham received what was promised."

Don't give up on God! Don't quit on the dreams God has given to you! Are you still waiting for one of God's promises to transpire? Perhaps you are waiting on God to give you wisdom, reconcile a relationship, heal a physical ailment, or provide a job for you. Chances are good that most of us are waiting on God to answer a prayer. This advice is easier to give than to receive, but be patient. God is faithful to accomplish what he promised to do. You can count on him. If you get impatient, you could miss the blessings God has in store for you.

RESPONDER'S REFLECTION: Sometimes we have a lot of patience because we don't use any of it. Many of the mistakes we make are simply because we got impatient waiting on God.

NOVEMBER 10TH

Isaiah 54:17 — "No weapon forged against you will prevail."

Politics at work can't stop you. A friend knifing you in the back can't stop you. Being turned down for a promotion can't stop you. Having too many bills and not enough money can't stop you. Making some detrimental life choices can't stop you. Getting injured or sick can't stop you. Losing what was once a valuable relationship can't stop you. Hearing hurtful words can't stop you. Friend, the Bible states in today's verse, "No weapon forged against you will prevail." God's Word says it, and that settles it.

RESPONDER'S REFLECTION: The only thing that can stop you, is you. Don't give up!

NOVEMBER 11TH

1 Samuel 30:6 — "But David found strength in the Lord his God."

Where do you find strength to face trials? Do you need more miracle-working power in your life today? You can find the strength you need when you look in the right place. Real strength isn't found in money, position, or even in the favor of others. True, life-altering strength can only be found in God. David was able to kill Goliath because he found strength in God and moved in his power instead of his own. If you want breakthrough power, make sure that God is your source of strength!

RESPONDER'S REFLECTION: You didn't come this far to come this far. You can walk in God's strength and power today.

NOVEMBER 12TH

Hebrews 10:17 — "Their sins and lawless acts I will remember no more."

One of the greatest miracles God has ever done is forgetting our sins. When we confess our sins and mistakes to God, he not only forgives us, but he chooses not to remember those offenses! Wow! If that good news doesn't get you excited, nothing can! What is the point? If God has forgotten about our worst sins and failings, shouldn't we forget them as well? If God, with his unlimited power and love, leaves our sins in the past, shouldn't we? The answer to those questions is yes!

RESPONDER'S REFLECTION: Don't bring up what God has forgotten. Don't keep a record of something that God isn't keeping track of. God doesn't want you focused on your past he wants you focused on Jesus past! Because of Jesus dying on the cross you are free!

NOVEMBER 13TH

Psalm 76:9 — "When you, God, rose up to judge."

We all need to learn and understand that there are two great spiritual truths: There is a God and we are not him! This fact is good to know because it helps us realize that God is the only one who judges our lives. My brother Ron said it best, "Put your finger on your nose and whosever nose you are touching should be the only person's business you should be in." We need to keep our eyes of judgment off others and be concerned about our own affairs. Nothing good ever comes from being judgmental and involving ourselves in other people's business.

RESPONDER'S REFLECTION: Stay out of other people's business unless they invite you into their business.

NOVEMBER 14TH

Matthew 19:26 — "With God all things are possible."

It always seems impossible until it happens! This year, the impossible can happen in your life. This year, a dramatic reversal can take place in your finances. This year, a breakthrough can start in your relationships. This year, your dreams can become a reality. However, notice the first word of today's verse is "with." The impossible is only possible "with" God. As you go through this year, experience every situation, second, and season "with" God.

RESPONDER'S REFLECTION: It always seems impossible until it happens. Nothing is impossible "with" God.

NOVEMBER 15TH

Hebrews 10:36 — "You need to persevere so that when you have done the will of God, you will receive what he has promised."

Successful people persevere and accomplish the seemingly impossible tasks of life because they never give up. They never buckle under the pressure of life's challenges. Despite the intensity of opposition, the overwhelming obstacles, and the mounting criticism, they persevere with determined resolve. They refuse to throw in the towel. Race car driver Rick Mears says it best, "*To finish first, you must first finish.*" Don't give up!

RESPONDER'S REFLECTION: The world is full of starters and short on finishers. Be a finisher in whatever you start.

NOVEMBER 16TH

Hebrews 12:1 —"Let us throw off everything that hinders and the sin that so easily entangles. And let us run with perseverance the race marked out for us."

God wants us to run the race of life with perseverance and to be blessed! Notice that with God's power, we can throw off everything that hinders us and the sins and mistakes that ensnare us. Today, throw off any hurt caused by the harsh words someone spoke over your life. Throw off the pain from the past, your fear of failure, low self-esteem, or anything else that is hindering you. With God's power, you can throw everything off so that you are free to run the race God has set for you.

RESPONDER'S REFLECTION: We can't run the race and have the victory and favor God wants us to have if we are holding onto things that are hindering us. Throw off your hindrances at Jesus' feet and be the champion God has called you to be.

NOVEMBER 17TH

Hebrews 13:8 —"Jesus Christ is the same yesterday and today and forever."

A lot has changed in this world! Cars that were once only gas operated can also now run on electricity. Many people have replaced their telephone landlines with a cellphone. You can communicate all over the world with one click. Most of us no longer use paper maps but have a GPS system in our car instead. On the other hand, Jesus has not changed. Jesus will always forgive our sins, heal our hearts, hear our prayers, and love us. In this ever-changing world of uncertainty, don't forget, "Jesus Christ is the same yesterday and today and forever."

RESPONDER'S REFLECTION: Great is the faithfulness of God! God is faithful when we aren't.

NOVEMBER 18TH

James 1:2 — "Consider it pure joy, my brothers and sisters, whenever you face trials of many kinds."

This verse can be difficult to accept at times because how do we consider trials a joy? Most of us dread trials and are disheartened by them. However, we can have joy in the midst of our troubles for several reasons:

1. God is with us in our trials, and will never leave or forsake us (Joshua 1:5).
2. God will love us through the trials (1 John 3:1).
3. God will help us overcome trials of all kinds (Romans 8:37).

Remember that joy is a choice, so despite the trials you may face today; choose to have the joy of the Lord!

RESPONDER'S REFLECTION: Happiness in life is temporary and is tied into our circumstances and mood. Joy in life is based on the eternal, and is tied into our walk with Jesus Christ.

NOVEMBER 19TH

Luke 4:18 — "The oppressed will be set free."

You will never overcome something you tolerate! God doesn't want you in bondage to anxiety, fear, worry, or anything else that would harm you. However, if you want or need God's help in any area of your life, you have to submit to him. God desires that you would rule and reign in life through his grace. However, if you are tolerating negative or sinful influences in your life, you are sabotaging your own destiny. God wants you free!

RESPONDER'S REFLECTION: You will never overcome something you tolerate.

NOVEMBER 20TH

2 Timothy 1:7 — "For the Spirit God gave us does not make us timid, but gives us power."

Timid, according to *Webster's Dictionary*, means easily frightened. Friend, God doesn't want you to live in fear; he wants you to live in faith. God doesn't want you to retreat from life but to attack it. If you want an abundant life of favor, peace, and blessing, you cannot be timid about it. People who get defeated in life feed their fear. People who have overwhelming victory in life feed their faith. The choice is up to you.

RESPONDER'S REFLECTION: What causes you to be afraid? Instead of feeding those fears, choose to feed your faith!

NOVEMBER 21ST

1 Corinthians 10:13 — "And God is faithful; he will not let you be tempted beyond what you can bear."

Everyone is tempted, but not everyone gives in to temptation. Today, if you are being tempted, realize that you don't have to give in to that temptation. The devil knows your Achilles' heel and he will attempt to exploit your weaknesses by making suggestions to entice you. But God wants you to have his supernatural power to overcome any temptation you face. Understand that whatever you are going through today, God has a way out!

RESPONDER'S REFLECTION: Don't try to face your temptation; run from it.

NOVEMBER 22ND

1 Peter 2:3 — "Now that you have tasted that the Lord is good."

Life can be tough sometimes, but that doesn't mean God isn't good. When we experience a difficult season in life, we might ask the question, "How can God allow this to happen?" Friend, as you go through life today, you can know that God is good even in the worst of times because he promises his peace (John 14:1), his healing (Psalm 147:3), his love (1 John 3:1), and his power (Luke 1:37). God is good all the time!

RESPONDER'S REFLECTION: Just because life can be tough doesn't mean that God isn't good.

NOVEMBER 23RD

1 Peter 1:2 — "Grace and peace be yours in abundance."

Today's verse is encouraging because the Creator of the entire universe wants us to have grace and peace in our life. In addition, God wants us to have these qualities in abundance. However, we need to understand that grace and peace can only come from God, and not this world. If we are not careful, the things of this world can actually do the opposite by robbing us of the very peace God desires for us. Today as you go about the business of life, submit to God so that he can give you his grace and peace in abundance.

RESPONDER'S REFLECTION: What you submit to, you will be full of in your life. If you submit to anger, you will be full of anger. If you submit to grace, you will be full of grace.

NOVEMBER 24TH

Psalm 147:3 — "He heals the brokenhearted and binds up their wounds."

For many people, the holidays are a fun time of the year centered on food, family gatherings, and football. However, for many others, the holidays can be a difficult time due to the loss of a loved one. During this time of year, we need to be sensitive to those who are grieving and brokenhearted. Sometimes, we can accidentally hurt those who are suffering by using Bible bullets, which are well-intentioned words that are cliché or unhelpful when we don't truly fathom the depth of loss that person is experiencing. Friend, when people are going through sorrow, the clichés don't help. However, we can help and give comfort to the brokenhearted by simply loving and listening to them.

RESPONDER'S REFLECTION: Life-changing ministry can take place when we simply listen with love to those who are hurting.

NOVEMBER 25TH

James 4:6 — "But he gives us more grace."

In life, we aren't going to be perfect in our marriages, parenting, and every-day living, but God's Word gives us a promise that "he gives us more grace." Although God wants us to avoid sin and evil in our lives, also realize that when we mess up, he gives us more grace. Romans 5:20 states, "But where sin increased, grace increased all the more." Therefore, never feel like you have wandered too far away from God to return. The grace of God is greater than any failure you have experienced.

RESPONDER'S REFLECTION: Mature Christians give grace to those who are struggling with sin while immature Christians give judgment. Which are you?

NOVEMBER 26TH

John 3:16 — "For God so loved the world."

There are days when I don't feel 100%. Sometimes, I wake up on the wrong side of bed where I feel cranky and irritable. But, do you know what is so amazing about God's love? His love is not dependent on my mood. God's love is not dependent on whether I am having a good or bad day. His love is unconditional and he loves me regardless of how I feel or act. God's love is always consistent and present. Today, rest in God's amazing love for you!

RESPONDER'S REFLECTION: If you want to flourish in life, you must understand how much God loves you regardless of how you feel or what you are doing.

NOVEMBER 27TH

2 Corinthians 5:7 — "For we live by faith, not by sight."

God has great plans for your life! I often remind people of this fact because many settle for less than God's best in their lives. Some people who struggle with life-controlling issues may believe the lie that life won't get much better. *However, God doesn't call us to live out a fact walk but a faith walk.* The fact might be that you are dealing with an addiction, but when you submit to God, he will help you overcome it if you walk in faith. Walking in faith requires risk, but it is a risk worth taking. Today, step out in faith and let God's amazing plans be fulfilled in your life!

RESPONDER'S REFLECTION: God does not call us to live out a fact walk but a faith walk.

NOVEMBER 28TH

Psalm 118:24 — "The Lord has done it this very day; let us rejoice today and be glad."

Even though life isn't always fair, this verse teaches that since God has given us this day to live, we should rejoice! I once heard someone say, *"You may not be able to control every situation and its outcome, but you can control your attitude."* Charles Swindoll states it another way, "Life is 10% what happens to you and 90% how you react to it." The bottom line is regardless of the issues that are going on in your life today; choose to rejoice because God has given you the gifts of his love and this day.

RESPONDER'S REFLECTION: My response is my responsibility. You can't control every situation going on around you, but you can control your response.

NOVEMBER 29TH

John 14:27 — "Peace I (Jesus) leave with you; my peace I give you."

God wants you to have peace, but in order to receive it, you need to relinquish control of your life! The only way we can have peace in our relationships, jobs, families, and lives is to yield to God and let him be the manager of our lives. Today, receive the peace of God and let go of those things in your life that are hurting you and keeping you from God's very best!

RESPONDER'S REFLECTION: You won't have peace if you always have to be in control of your life.

NOVEMBER 30TH

John 6:12 —"When they had all had enough to eat, he said to his disciples, 'Gather the pieces that are left over. Let nothing be wasted.'"

Today's verse is referring to the story where Jesus took five loaves of bread, two fish and miraculously fed thousands. There are three remarkable lessons we can learn:

1. God understands our every need and takes care of us.
2. God uses the small things we are willing to give to him and then multiplies them.
3. God always gives in abundance.

After Jesus fed the five thousand people, it was amazing to discover that twelve baskets of food were left over by those who had eaten that day.

RESPONDER'S REFLECTION: Never forget that little is much when it is in God's hand.

DECEMBER 1ST

John 5:8 —"Then Jesus said to him, 'Get up! Pick up your mat and walk.'"

Have you heard the expression, *"God helps those who help themselves"?* In today's verse, the exact opposite occurs between Jesus and the man in this story. Earlier in the chapter, a man who had a disability for thirty-eight years tried to get into a healing pool to get relief for his lame body, but every time he attempted to enter the pool, someone else always got ahead of him. This man could not help himself. Today some of us have tried, but we can't help ourselves either. The good news isn't that *God helps those who help themselves, but instead, God helps those who CAN'T help themselves.* Let him help you today!

RESPONDER'S REFLECTION: The good news is God helps those who can't help themselves because he has amazing love and compassion toward us!

DECEMBER 2ND

Exodus 14:14 — "The Lord will fight for you; you need only to be still."

At times, we all have battles we must face in life. However, God wants to fight those battles on our behalf, but we need to let him. In fact, the Bible says that we need to "be still." Why would God ask us to be still when we are going through our trials? Because he is Almighty God and has full power to deal with all problems that come our way. When we are still, we get out of God's way and trust him to take care of the situation. The good news is God knows exactly what we need, so we can **be still** and rest in the fact that God will get us through the battles of life.

RESPONDER'S REFLECTION: When we force ourselves to be still, it is a sign to God that we trust him. It is also a sign to others that you trust God to fight for you!

DECEMBER 3RD

John 11:35 — "Jesus wept."

Have you ever felt like nobody cared about or understood you? Most people have heard the phrase, "Jesus loves you." However, what I love about today's short verse is it demonstrates the compassion Jesus has for us through his shed tears rather than just telling us. In this story from John 11, the heart of Jesus was moved so much that he wept. The good news is that Jesus' heart is also moved with compassion for you. God loves you more than you can know!

RESPONDER'S REFLECTION: God loves you so much that his heart is moved with compassion for you!

DECEMBER 4TH

John 9:3 — "This happened so that the works of God might be displayed in him."

Do you ever wonder why problems even happen in the first place? In this story, the disciples are trying to understand why a man was born with the physical ailment of blindness. Jesus' response to them was, "**This happened so that the works of God might be displayed in him**." To apply this verse to your own life, you need to realize that the troubles you are facing shouldn't be viewed as problems, but instead as opportunities for God to display his power in your life. Today, try to change your perspective from viewing problems as problems to now regarding them as opportunities.

RESPONDER'S REFLECTION: You can't change your destiny until you change your outlook! We may see trials that give us pain. God sees tests that give us the opportunity for promotion!

DECEMBER 5TH

Exodus 14:13 – "But Moses told the people," Don't be afraid. Just stand still and watch the Lord rescue you today."

This verse comes from the story of Moses leading God's people out of captivity in Egypt. Moses had led God's people away from Pharaoh, who had the most powerful army in the world. The only problem was now God's people were boxed in because Pharaoh's army was behind them and the Red Sea was in front of them. Why could Moses so calmly tell the people not to be afraid? Because Moses understood one very important truth that if God brings you to it, he will bring your through it! Today, if you are between a rock and a hard place just know that you are not alone.

RESPONDER'S REFLECTION: If God brings you to it, he will bring you through it!

DECEMBER 6TH

Colossians 3:23 — "Whatever you do, work at it with all your heart, as working for the Lord, not for human masters."

In the words of Hall of Fame Coach Vince Lombardi, "The only place success comes before work is in the dictionary." Sometimes we expect God to do everything while we just sit back and do nothing. Of course, God desires to work, move, and minister on our behalf. However, we need to take responsibility and be good stewards of what God has given to us. Whatever God has called you to do today, go full throttle and work at it with all your heart. Remember, that God has big plans for your life!

RESPONDER'S REFLECTION: Men and women who have accomplished great things for God have done so by partnering with him. Partnership means both sides have responsibility!

DECEMBER 7TH

Isaiah 55:8 — "'For my thoughts are not your thoughts, neither are your ways my ways,' declares the Lord."

Recently, I was earnestly praying about a situation in my life. However, the answer I received from God regarding my request was no. To be honest, I don't like to hear the word no. As I stepped back from the situation, I suddenly started to remember how upset I would get in the past if God answered no to my requests. Then years later, I would look back and realize how grateful I was that God did not give me what I thought I wanted. If God has told you no to a request, understand that he sees your life from the beginning to the end. He sees the big picture and has our best interests at heart even when the answer is no. As difficult as it may seem, we just need to trust that he always knows what is best for us.

RESPONDER'S REFLECTION: Sometimes the greatest answer God can give to our prayer request is no.

DECEMBER 8TH

Matthew 5:45 — "He sends rain on the righteous and the unrighteous."

Life is not always going to be fair! There is no verse in the Bible where God says that life is fair. When treated unfairly, you really only have two choices: You can become either a victim or a student. The victim will grumble, complain, and blame other people for their misfortune. On the other hand, the student will try to figure out how they can learn and grow from the unfortunate painful situation. When life treats you unfairly, will you be a victim or a student? Those who make the tough choice to be a student are the ones who will change the world!

RESPONDERS REFLECTION: When life is unfair to you, how will you respond? Will you be a victim or a student?

DECEMBER 9TH

Joshua 1:5 — "I will never leave you nor forsake you."

The dictionary defines abandon as *to desert*. I have known friends whose spouses and parents have deserted them, but God won't ever abandon us. An amazing fact about God never leaving us is that he knows all the sins and mistakes we have committed and still chooses to stay with us. Conversely, the reason my friends were deserted was due to the mistakes they made. God has seen *every* sin, yet he refuses not to desert us. He cares for us beyond what we can fully comprehend.

RESPONDER'S REFLECTION: The promises of God don't have power in our lives until we start to believe them. Understand and believe that God won't leave you!

DECEMBER 10TH

John 14:27 —"Peace I leave with you; my peace I give you. I do not give to you as the world gives."

As Christmas is approaching, many children excitedly wait in expectation to see what gifts they will receive. In today's verse, we see that God wants to give us the gift of his peace in our heart and minds. What makes God's gifts so great is they aren't like the ones the world gives because they never break, tarnish, or need replacing. Today, receive the gifts God has given you and don't leave them unopened.

RESPONDER'S REFLECTION: God wants to give us gifts. However, when we don't get what God wants us to have, the issue isn't with the giving, but with the receiving. Today, receive all that God has for you!

DECEMBER 11TH

Psalm 26:5 —"I abhor the assembly of evildoers and refuse to sit with the wicked."

Aren't there times we all wish we could say this verse about ourselves? We have the ability to choose righteousness or wickedness, but sadly, there are times when we choose to do evil. How do we stop ourselves from doing evil? The simple response is to refuse to associate with wickedness. **Refuse** to give into that temptation to lust, steal, lie, or any other sin. Today, **refuse** to go along with the crowd, especially if they are doing wrong. When you take a stand for righteousness and do what God wants you to do, you will never be in the minority because he is with you!

RESPONDER'S REFLECTION: Refuse to give into sin. Refuse to give up on God. Refuse to stop believing for the blessings of God over your life!

DECEMBER 12TH

Exodus 34:6-7 — "The Lord, the Lord, the compassionate and gracious God, slow to anger, abounding in love and faithfulness, maintaining love to thousands, and forgiving wickedness, rebellion and sin."

This passage of scripture is amazing because God is so wonderfully describing himself. Sadly, many people have an inaccurate view of God as a strict judge or they see him through the lens of being like their imperfect earthly father. Friend, God truly is compassionate and merciful and he lavishly pours out his love and forgiveness to all of us. Today, if the lens you view God through is clouded by your mistakes or misunderstanding of God, then let the truth of God's love clear up your view!

RESPONDER'S REFLECTION: The love of God cannot be stopped by any army, people, or nation.

DECEMBER 13TH

Joshua 24:15 — "But if serving the Lord seems undesirable to you, then choose for yourselves this day whom you will serve."

Change is inevitable! If we are honest with ourselves, we know there are changes we need to make in our lives. However, there is a difference between knowing we need to change and actually implementing that change in our life. The problem is many times, we miss God's point regarding change in our life. A wise man once said, *"You make the choice and God makes the change."* In other words, when we choose to serve God, he is the One who begins to make changes in us. The power to change only comes when we repeatedly make healthy choices.

RESPONDER'S REFLECTION: You can't change your life without making healthy choices. If your choices aren't healthy, then your life won't be either.

DECEMBER 14TH

Psalm 21:1 — "How great is his joy in the victories you give!"

Are you settling for an average, run-of-the-mill life? What areas of your life are you tolerating to have less than God's best? God wants to give us his victory! However, in order for us to grab ahold of God's blessings and victory, we have to release all the second bests we have held onto. You don't have to settle for second best in any area of your life! Today, seize God's very best for your life and leave behind the mediocre and mundane!

RESPONDER'S REFLECTION: Receiving everything God wants you to have requires having the courage to wait. Anybody can settle for mediocre. However, it truly takes courage to wait on God's very best!

DECEMBER 15TH

John 3:16 — "For God so loved the world that he gave his one and only Son, that whoever believes in him shall not perish but have eternal life."

Your life is valuable! In fact, it is so valuable that God gave his son, Jesus, so you would not perish but have eternal life. Today, if you are struggling with low self-esteem, those feelings are not from God. God regards you as highly valued! No matter what mistakes you have made or regardless of what you have accomplished, God thinks your life is incredibly important. Today, realize that God not only loves you, but he values and cherishes you!

RESPONDER'S REFLECTION: You will flourish in life when you truly comprehend how much God loves you. You can't make sense out of any part of life until you understand that you are the object of God's love!

DECEMBER 16TH

Psalm 27:1 — "The Lord is my light and my salvation."

Have you ever hurt yourself stumbling around in the dark? Of course, this experience only happens if you enter a room and don't turn on the light. When we make decisions without first consulting God in prayer or reading the Bible, it is exactly like entering that dark room except that we can damage a lot more than our physical bodies. Today, turn the light on in your relationships, finances, job, or any other area. When you ask God for his wisdom, he will direct your steps.

RESPONDER'S REFLECTION: There are wise human counselors, but they can only give you wisdom based on what they know, which is limited. God is the best counselor because he can give you wisdom based on the fact that he sees your entire past, present, and future.

DECEMBER 17TH

Psalm 31:24 — "Be strong and take heart, all you who hope in the Lord."

Courage isn't a subject you hear preached on very often, but since it is important to God, it should be to us as well. It takes courage to do the right thing. Likewise, it takes courage to say no to the wrong thing. Every day, we face choices that present us with either taking the high road or the low road. Today, as you make choices regarding your money, faith, family, or marriage, have the courage to make the right choices!

RESPONDER'S REFLECTION: Walking in courage doesn't mean the absence of fear, but it means despite the presence of fear, we continue to move forward.

DECEMBER 18TH

Proverbs 26:12—"Do you see a person wise in their own eyes? There is more hope for a fool than for them."

If we are not careful, pride can easily seep into our lives. Anytime we allow ourselves to become prideful, we are guaranteed to have problems. A good friend of mine who works in law enforcement once said, "Humility breeds capability." This expression is so true in law enforcement and every area of life. When we humble ourselves and say sincere prayers such as, "God, I need your help in my marriage" or "God, help me to be the person you want me to be" or "God, I messed up, please turn this situation around," God will begin to move in our lives. When we humbly go to God with our needs, he is capable of working on our behalf and giving us his supernatural help.

RESPONDER'S REFLECTION: The more you pray, the more humble you are whereas the less you pray, the more prideful you are. When we don't spend time in prayer, we are actually sending a message to God that we don't need him.

DECEMBER 19TH

Psalm 30:11 —"You turned my wailing into dancing."

Are you feeling sad or depressed today? An important word in this verse is *you because it is referring* to God himself. God is the only One who has the power to turn our mourning into dancing. We may turn to other things such as money, promotions, or drugs/medications, but only the power and love of God is what turns our mourning into dancing. God's love gives us a joy that can never be taken away.

RESPONDER'S REFLECTION: God turns our problems into opportunities, our bondages into blessings, and our tragedies into triumphs.

DECEMBER 20TH

Philippians 4:13 — "I can do all this through him who gives me strength."

If this verse doesn't get you excited, I am not sure anything will. God is reminding us of the fact that we can do all things through him. However, sometimes we speak negatively about ourselves and the situations we are experiencing that we inadvertently derail our own lives and vision. For example, if you say to yourself, "I can't do it" then more than likely you won't be able to do it. Today, I want to encourage you to begin speaking positive words and most importantly, God's Word over your life. Remember that you can do everything through Christ!

RESPONDER'S REFLECTION: If you want less of God's power, repeat what the devil says about you. If you want more of God's power, repeat what God says about you.

DECEMBER 21ST

Psalm 28:9 — "Be their shepherd and carry them forever."

God does many wonderful things, but the two mentioned in today's verse are my favorites. First, he is our shepherd, which means he leads us. God gives us his wisdom and direction when we seek him. Secondly, he carries us in his loving arms when we are overwhelmed. If you are encountering stress, maybe it is time to stop wearing yourself out and allow the arms of your loving Father to carry you. First Responders are always helping others and oftentimes struggle the most to receive help when they need it. Therefore, we need to allow God to lead and carry us because that is something he wants to do for us!

RESPONDER'S REFLECTION: The battles we face in our lives belong to the Lord, so give him all those battles and he will carry you through it!

DECEMBER 22ND

Psalm 32:5 —"And you forgave the guilt of my sin."

This verse is an amazing example of how God is able to do what no one else can do. At times, we have all hurt someone and asked them to forgive us. Yet, even when others forgive us, they can't remove our guilt. However, God has the power not only forgive to us, but also to remove the guilt and shame of our sins. Today, if you have confessed your sin to God and asked him to forgive you, but you still struggle with feelings of guilt, this is not God's will. God desires to remove ALL your guilt, and he is the only One who can and will do it!

RESPONDER'S REFLECTION: If you have truly repented and asked God to forgive you, but you hear a condemning voice telling you otherwise, I promise that voice is not from God. The devil wants you consumed with guilt, but God wants you filled with his grace.

DECEMBER 23RD

Psalm 37:23 —"The Lord makes firm the steps of the one who delights in him."

Many times, we know to share our big prayer requests with God, such as asking him to save a loved one's life or heal a relationship. However, frequently we don't share with God the little requests because we think they are too small to bring to him or that other things are more important. Friend, no matter how small or trivial the issues are in your life, if they bother you, take those requests to God in prayer. God is not only concerned with the big situations in our lives, but also the smaller ones as well.

RESPONDER'S REFLECTION: God wants a loving father and child relationship with you, not a business relationship. If something small is bothering you, take it to God because he wants to help you.

DECEMBER 24TH

Matthew 6:33 —"But seek first his kingdom and his righteousness, and all these things will be given to you as well."

All of us have priorities, but we don't always have them in order. The truth is that w*hen your priorities are wrong, many times, you are the last person to realize it.* Did you catch that? Friend, when we make it our main priority to honor God with our lives, that one goal will bless our relationships, finances, work situations, and absolutely every area of our existence. However, when we mess up our priorities, we end up harming everything we value. Today, remember to seek first his kingdom!

RESPONDER'S REFLECTION: When your priorities are wrong, you are the last person to realize it.

DECEMBER 25TH

Isaiah 7:14 —"Therefore the Lord himself will give you a sign: The virgin will conceive and give birth to a son, and will call him Immanuel."

Christmastime is a blessing as we reflect upon and thank God for the birth of his precious son, Jesus! Yet unfortunately, for some people, Christmas can be a tough reminder of lost loved ones, painful issues, relationship problems, or other hurtful experiences. Christmas is merry because Jesus came into this world to:

1. Rescue and redeem us from our sins.
2. Save us from ourselves.
3. Give us hope and be a light in our dark circumstances.
4. Heal our hurts, habits, and hang-ups.

On this day, remember that you are so important to God that he gave his son, Jesus for you. Merry Christmas!

RESPONDER'S REFEDCTOIN: Christ came into the world to heal hearts and set people free.

DECEMBER 26TH

Joshua 1:9 — "For the Lord your God will be with you wherever you go."

This verse can be viewed as both scary and comforting at the same time. When we start going down the wrong path and give in to lust, lying, gossiping, or any other sin, God is with us and sees every mistake we make. Yet, thankfully, we can turn to him and repent and he will forgive us. For the comforting side of this verse, when we experience the trials of life such as death, loss, divorce, and abandonment, God is there with us through it all. If you are doing things you shouldn't, repent and receive the lavish love of God. If you are going through a trial, you don't need to search for God because he is always right there with you.

RESPONDER'S REFLECTION: We won't know until we get to heaven how many instances the presence of God has been with us and protected us from the dangers we never knew were there.

DECEMBER 27TH

Psalm 46:1 — "God is our refuge and strength, an ever-present help in trouble."

Are you a morning person? I definitely am not! Coffee is my best friend. When Kelly and I were first married, I told her that I didn't want to have any serious conversations in the morning because it takes some time before I am awake and alert. One of my favorite things about God is that he is always awake and ready to help us in times of trouble. Therefore, if you are encountering hardships today in any area of your life, the good news is God created coffee, but he doesn't need it to function early in the morning or late at night. He is an ever-present help to you anytime!

RESPONDER'S REFLECTION: You can go to God anytime of the day because he is always awake and ready to help you!

DECEMBER 28TH

Psalm 42:11 —"Why, my soul, are you downcast? Why so disturbed within me? Put your hope in God, for I will yet praise him, my Savior and my God."

Are you feeling discouraged or sad? If you aren't right now, chances are you will experience those feelings later on in life. When our soul is downcast and sad, it is because we may have forgotten or lost track of the truth that God is in control. At times, we can lose sight of the fact that regardless of the predicament we are in, God can get us out and turn things around. Sometimes we make the mistake of projecting our own limitations on to God. The good news is God is limitless so we can put our hope in him to help us through any trial in life. So, why be discouraged?

RESPONDER'S REFLECTION: When God is in control of our lives, we have more peace. On the contrary, when we have to be in control, the result leaves us feeling downcast and discouraged.

DECEMBER 29TH

Exodus 3:4 —"God called to him from within the bush, "Moses! Moses"

If the Lord can get your attention he can exceed your expectation! In Exodus 3 God is crying out to Moses. God used a burning bush to try to get Moses attention. Maybe today God is using some trial or situation to get your attention. Once God got Moses attention he gave him a plan to save hundreds of thousands of lives. God wants your attention so that he can do something incredible in your life! Don't be distracted today by pain, success, loss, or discouragements. God has something big in store for you. We can never do the incredible works of God without first being led by God.

RESPONDER'S REFLECTION: If the Lord can get your attention he can exceed your expectation. Today if something is distracting you from God it is time to turn that off and turn your attention to Jesus.

DECEMBER 30TH

Matthew 5:45 — "He sends rain on the just and the unjust alike."

Life is not fair! Nowhere in the Bible does God mention that life is fair. When something unjust happens to you, you only have two choices. You can become a victim or a student. The victim starts grumbling, complaining, and blaming other people for what has happened to them. The student looks to see how they can learn and grow from the unfortunate painful situation. When life is unfair to you, will you choose to be a victim or a student? Those who make the tough choice to be a student are the ones who change the world!

RESPONDER'S REFLECTION: When life is unfair to you, how will you respond?

DECEMBER 31ST

2 Corinthians 5:17 — "Therefore, if anyone is in Christ, the new creation has come: The old has gone, the new is here!"

Today is the last day of the year! During this time, we tend to reflect on this past year and happily say goodbye to all the hurtful situations and things we don't like or want in our life. However, with a new year approaching, it is also a great time to look ahead with anticipation. Let's look forward to how we can partner with God to make our dreams come true. Friend, with the help of God, cut off your sins, mistakes, and past failures, and believe him to give you a supernatural year of his favor and blessing! God is giving you a new year with a new start!

RESPONDER'S REFLECTION: With the power of God, give the gift of goodbye to hurtful situations, past sins, failures, and anything else that is negatively affecting your life. This upcoming year is your year of God's blessing and favor!

Books by Barry Young

"30 Second Devotional"

"30 Second Devotional for First Responders"

"How to Have Victory in Life"

"How to Live a Life of Blessing"

To learn more about Barry Young
or Serving Pastors Ministries
visit www.servingpastors.com